CTRL+ALT+ DELETE

I0139533

Anthony Clarvoe

BROADWAY PLAY PUBLISHING INC
New York
www.broadwayplaypublishing.com
info@broadwayplaypublishing.com

CTRL+ALT+DELETE
© Copyright 2005 by Anthony Clarvoe

Cover photo by T Charles Erickson

First printing: July 2005
This printing: November 2015
I S B N: 978-88145-254-9

Book design: Marie Donovan
Word processing: Microsoft Word
Typographic controls: Xerox Ventura Publisher 2.0 P E
Typeface: Palatino
Printed and bound in the U S A

CTRL+ALT+DELETE was commissioned by the Wharton Center for the Performing Arts. It was presented as a workshop by the Wharton Center, directed by the author; by South Coast Repertory in their NewSCRipts series, directed by Mark Rucker; and by San Jose Repertory Theatre, directed by Ethan McSweeny.

The world premiere of CTRL+ALT+DELETE was presented by San Jose Repertory Theatre (Timothy Near, Artistic Director, Alexandra Urbanowski, Managing Director) in a co-production with the Wharton Center for the Performing Arts (William Wright, Executive Director) on 26 October 2001. The cast and creative contributors were:

GUS BELMONT ....James Carpenter
TORIA BRUNO ....Jennifer Kato
EDDIE FISKER .... Patrick Darragh
MARIE .... Betsy Brandt
CARBURY GRENDALL ....Sam Gregory
TOM XEROX ....Robert Nagle

Director .... Ethan McSweeny
Set .... Todd Rosenthal
Lights .... Frances Aronson
Costumes ....B Modern
Sound ....Jeff Mockus
Stage manager ....Nina Iventosch

CTRL+ALT+DELETE was presented by George Street Playhouse (David Saint, Artistic Director, Michael Stotts, Managing Director) on March 22, 2002. The cast and creative contributors were:

GUS BELMONT . . . . Jonathan Hogan
TORIA BRUNO . . . . K J Sanchez
EDDIE FISKER . . . . James Ludwig
MARIE . . . . .Sarah Avery
CARBURY GRENDALL . . . . Sam Gregory
TOM XEROX . . . . .Daniel Pearce

Director . . . . Ethan McSweeny
Set . . . . Mark Wendland
Lights . . . . Jeff Croiter
Costumes . . . . Michael Sharpe
Sound . . . . Bruce Ellman
Stage manager . . . . Patti McCabe

CHARACTERS & SETTING

GUS BELMONT, *fifties, the money*
TORIA BRUNO, *thirties, a financial reporter*
EDDIE FISKER, *late twenties, an entrepreneur*
MARIE, *twenties, a "niece"*
CARBURY GRENDALL, *late thirties, the C E O*
TOM XEROX, *early thirties, marketing and sales*

Setting: Corporate America, 1998 to 2000: Convention centers, airport lounges, conference rooms, hotel rooms, a financial television network studio. Nowhere private. Nothing personal. Nobody's home.

STAGING NOTES

The set needs to be one sleek place that can be many places, sometimes several at once. There is no time to stop and move furniture. Scenes are established by how the characters behave and what they carry in, and by changes of sound and light. A character left onstage at the end of a scene is fast-forwarded to a different time and place by the entrance of fresh characters accompanied by new sound and light. These time and space warps are indicated in the script by the words "fast forward". A sound and light cue evoking this is helpful. Scenes are so continuous as to almost overlap.

A number of scenes take place among characters who, though they are sharing the same stage space, are in different geographical locations, talking to each other on their phones. The phones are always mobile, often headsets. The actors' paths may cross, but obviously they never touch in these scenes, and never make eye contact.

The characters see and respond to many things that are just outside the fourth wall and invisible to us, but no action called for in the script requires the use of mime, opening invisible doors and so on.

The point: these characters travel light and improvise. They do not need desks to work, they do not need big tables to meet around, they do not need beds to rest. They create the place they are by what they do.

ACKNOWLEDGMENTS

My thanks to the staff and board of the Wharton Center for the Performing Arts, the faculty and students of the Department of Theater, Michigan State University, and the community of East Lansing, Michigan for their hospitality and help during the writing of the play.

I am grateful to Dennis Romer, John Stefano, and the students of Otterbein College Theater for their contributions to the play during my residency there.

In addition to the above, thanks to Bill Craver for matchmaking; Jerry Patch and Liz Engelman for friendship and dramaturgy; and to M David Campbell II, Erna Clarvoe, Mitch Gaynor, Marita Grobbel, and Michael Knox and the people at Polyphasic, Inc. for patient answers to many questions.

ACT ONE

(GUS BELMONT *stands, holding a microphone. The stage at a corporate convention*)

BELMONT: First I want to thank you all for inviting me to kick off this shindig. I appreciate the chance to lay the rumors to rest. You've all heard about my little health adventure. Made me glad I gave all that seed money to those defibrillator people. Now I know folks are asking—what'll he do now? The man died on the table. The man had an out-of-body experience. Isn't he going to slow down? Well, some of you have heard this story, indulge me. They tell me I was lying there, hooked up to monitors, indicators crashing. I saw— I did—I saw that white light. Majestic beings beckoning me onward. Morgan, Rothschild. Calling me home. And I said...I said...oh, there's no way I'm going to die in the middle of a market like this! And they tell me— they tell me that at that moment! The Dow broke ten thousand. And I came to. In a whole new world of wealth. And I said, well, I'm not dead. So I must be free. Now people want to know what a heart attack will do to me? People are asking what dying on the table will do to me? People, this is the most alive any of us is ever going to be! And I've got a question for *you*. I came back from the dead to participate in this time. What are *you* going to do?

(*The lights fade to:*)

(TORIA BRUNO, *under lights. A T V studio*)

TORIA: This is Toria Bruno, at this hour the Dow is up one hundred sixty, if this holds it will be another record high, the Nasdaq continues to flirt with four thousand, it has made back all the ground it lost over the summer, just incredible, we've got quarterly consumer confidence numbers out this afternoon, we're tracking the latest round of mergers in telecom, the Word on the Street spotlight will be my exclusive interview with Prospera Funds' investment genius Gus Belmont and if you've been watching you know this is a big day for us. I am coming to you from our spiffy new studios—do we have the shot of the Big Ticker? Do we? The whole faade—can they see this?—the building is illuminated, there it is, that's live, you can see it's an illuminated quote board, running numbers all the time, I am broadcasting here from inside this skin of constantly renewed information, the, what, the life blood of the markets flowing over us and around us and I am at the nerve center and—well, we're pretty excited around here.

(A man, sitting, his face unseen behind the magazine he's reading, which has BELMONT's *face on the cover. An airport lounge)*

*(*EDDIE FISKER *enters, rolling a small suitcase and carrying a briefcase. He sees the man and stops. He crosses to the man.)*

EDDIE: Hi. Excuse me. Hi.

(The man lowers his magazine and looks at him. It is BELMONT *himself.)*

EDDIE: Mr Belmont?

BELMONT: *(Smiling wryly at the cover photo of himself)* You caught me reading pornography.

EDDIE: You must bump into yourself a lot like that.

BELMONT: I'm getting hard to avoid.

EDDIE: I wouldn't say that. You don't know how long it took to set up this meeting.

BELMONT: This one here?

EDDIE: No, I—the one I'm flying to.

BELMONT: Which is with me?

EDDIE: Hi, Eddie Fisker, I'm with J P Morgan, Mergers and Acquisitions. I just wanted to tell you how outstanding it was to hear you speak. The stuff about wireless, it's, I don't know, it's like you take my thoughts, these foggy random pictures in my head and just coalesce them, and shoom...You know?

BELMONT: Glad to be of help.

EDDIE: I should let you get back to your—

BELMONT: Have you got the pitch book with you? Whatever Morgan has you pitching to me?

EDDIE: Um. Kind of. I won't really be doing the pitching, I'm just a junior analyst, there are other people coming, bigger people...

BELMONT: Give it here.

EDDIE: My boss, my boss's boss...

BELMONT: But you did the analysis.

EDDIE: Yes, sir.

BELMONT: So why should I listen to your analysis from a bunch of empty suits?

EDDIE: That's a demonstration of our belief in this deal. Sending our most credible people.

BELMONT: They just don't get it, do they.

EDDIE: Uh...

BELMONT: I don't want credible. I want incredible. Credible makes a profit. Incredible makes a killing. Show me something incredible.

(Beat)

EDDIE: Okay. Here goes. *(Opening his briefcase, summoning his nerve, and handing* BELMONT *an elegant binder)* Okay. If you want me to, I can—

BELMONT: I can take myself through it.

EDDIE: But there's this big Power Point presentation.

BELMONT: Let's see it.

EDDIE: What?

BELMONT: On the laptop.

EDDIE: Um, you bet. *(Sitting next to* BELMONT *and opening his laptop)* The concept is total wireless connectivity, in your pocket. A platform that can handle all the ways people are trying to reach each other and everything they need to keep their lives together as they go through the day. Cell phone, pager, emailer, locator, organizer, all in one device. The Gizmo. Okay, first, you can see—

BELMONT: Yes I can. Next.

EDDIE: Okay. Now—

BELMONT: And the lines go up and up. What a surprise. Next.

EDDIE: Here...

BELMONT: Next. Next. Next.

EDDIE: If you have any questions...

BELMONT: No, thanks. This looks to me more like an idea than a going concern.

EDDIE: There's been product development, I could show you—

BELMONT: Seems pretty raw for a Morgan pitch.

EDDIE: The pace of these things is changing.

BELMONT: Is this your own idea here?

(Beat)

EDDIE: Yes, sir, it is.

BELMONT: Not a Morgan pitch at all.

EDDIE: Sir, I have been about this idea for two years now—

BELMONT: So you put it in a Morgan cover and handed it to me.

EDDIE: I carry it around in a Morgan cover, it deserves to be in a Morgan cover—

BELMONT: Does Morgan see it that way?

EDDIE: Morgan doesn't get it! And I saw you here and I know it isn't ready but I heard what you said, the world doesn't wait till you're ready, if there's anything here the man will see it.

BELMONT: So why are you at Morgan?

EDDIE: To meet you.

BELMONT: I'm not that hard to meet.

EDDIE: Oh, see, the people who get to meet you, they're all referred—

BELMONT: So?

EDDIE: So you don't know anybody who doesn't know somebody you already know! Good idea obviously, maximizes your time, but you are surrounded by gatekeepers, sir. The power of venture capital is that it breaks through the gatekeepers who stand between money and the people who will put it to its most exciting use.

BELMONT: I said that.

EDDIE: Yes, sir, you did. A long time ago.

BELMONT: A year ago.

EDDIE: Yeah, when the world was young.

BELMONT: I'm an accessible guy. You weren't tackled by bodyguards. Just a simple business traveler like yourself. Sitting with a magazine. Humbly.

EDDIE: All I mean is it must feel amazing to have that kind of confidence. Most people worry they're not connected enough. Which is why I'm developing the Gizmo. So maybe people like me might have the same kind of confidence as Gus Belmont.

(MARIE *enters.*)

MARIE: Sorry sorry sorry sorry sorry, we can go.

BELMONT: Did you get it?

MARIE: Come on, be nice. (*Picking up the magazine*) Hey, what's this?

BELMONT: Just seeing if they got the story straight.

MARIE: Uh huh. Seeing what you got away with.

BELMONT: So you both think I'm getting too full of myself.

EDDIE: No, oh, I never meant any—

MARIE: Too late, you're already full of yourself, you're overflowing all over everything.

BELMONT: The grief I get. (*As he stands, to* EDDIE) So where you flying to?

EDDIE: You tell me.

(*Beat*)

MARIE: Okay, this is so Biblical.

EDDIE: Mr Belmont. If you think my idea is...

BELMONT: Son, I think we both know your Gizmo is not really a credible idea.

EDDIE: Well, but...do you think it might be an incredible idea?

(Beat)

BELMONT: Let's talk on my plane. *(He exits.)*

EDDIE: On the plane. I'm on the plane. Hi. Eddie Fisker. I'm. That is my name. And I'm on the plane. Getting. With Mr Belmont. And you. Too. Hi. *(He kisses her full on the lips.)* Oh my God. I do not know who you are. I am so sorry.

MARIE: Happens all the time. Come on, keep up.

(MARIE exits. EDDIE frantically gathers his luggage. CARBURY GRENDALL enters and crosses to EDDIE. A corporate office conference room)

GRENDALL: So. I've got a new baby brother.

EDDIE: Hi.

GRENDALL: Whatever. Carbury Grendall.

EDDIE: I've heard about you.

GRENDALL: Why thanks. So way to go, you got your toe in the door. Now I get to see if you'd be a good investment, who you are, what you're made of. Shouldn't take long.

EDDIE: Why you?

GRENDALL: A question I ask myself.

EDDIE: I mean I only know what I read in the *Journal*, but—

GRENDALL: But aren't I vastly overqualified to be messing in your business.

EDDIE: Took the words right out of my—

GRENDALL: I thank you. After the events you read about—

EDDIE: You cratered your startup, is that right?

GRENDALL: I did not crater my startup!

EDDIE: My mistake.

GRENDALL: Belmont offered me a gig here at Prospera, Entrepreneur In Residence deal, look around for my next shebang, do some chores, wax the car. Take out the garbage. It's the least he could do.

EDDIE: Because?

GRENDALL: Another time. And that includes the due diligence on you.

EDDIE: And?

GRENDALL: And I'm impressed.

EDDIE: You like the idea?

GRENDALL: I like your nerve, trying to pass off this half-baked piece of sheetcake as a going concern. We're a business incubator, not a Suzie Homemaker Oven, okay?

EDDIE: Okay.

GRENDALL: Just stay on your side of the room and don't touch my toys, we'll get along fine. Now let's get cracking.

EDDIE: What are your toys?

GRENDALL: I'll tell you when you touch them.

(MARIE *peeks in.*)

MARIE: Have you guys seen Himself?

GRENDALL: There's one of them now.

EDDIE: Really.

MARIE: Sorry sorry sorry.

GRENDALL: Try the lap pool.

MARIE: He's not in the lap pool, he disappeared and he didn't tell me and he must have turned off his cell—

GRENDALL: Try the television.

MARIE: I checked, he's not watching the television—

GRENDALL: No, he might be on the television. Let's see.

(GRENDALL *points a remote. Lights up on* BELMONT *and* TORIA *in her T V studio*)

MARIE: There he is, oh my God.

(*During the following* GRENDALL *opens a laptop and points and clicks as he watches the T V.*)

TORIA: Gus Belmont, you have been called the Titan of the Tech Sector, the Seer, the—

BELMONT: Here we go—

MARIE: Eeyoo. Who is she?

TORIA: The Man With the Crystal Balls—

BELMONT: Every time I'm on here—

GRENDALL: That's Toria Bruno—

TORIA: I don't make this up—

GRENDALL: Where have you been?

MARIE: Cash poor.

TORIA: The Biggest Basket in this Super Market—

BELMONT: Oh, for—who says this stuff?

TORIA: In the chat rooms, on the trading floors—

MARIE: This isn't good for him.

TORIA: You are The Market Guru.

BELMONT: Now, I don't like that term.

MARIE: Oh, that one you don't like.

BELMONT: Right after they call you that, they start cutting you down.

TORIA: Speaking of cutting you down, it looked like we'd lost you for a while there.

BELMONT: But I beat it. All better.

TORIA: That's great. We're all grateful.

MARIE: You ego whore!

TORIA: Up next, the Pick of the Week.

GRENDALL: Here we go.

TORIA: This week, what Gus Belmont thinks is hot and ready to catch fire.

GRENDALL: *(Poised at the laptop)* Ready, set...

BELMONT: Wireless.

GRENDALL: *(Furiously working his laptop)* And they're off.

TORIA: We'll be right back.

(Lights down on TORIA *and* BELMONT*)*

EDDIE: *(Looking over* GRENDALL*'s shoulder)* Day trading?

GRENDALL: Of course not, we're on company time. *(Day trading busily)* Wireless. I told him that. I've been saying that forever.

*(*MARIE*'s phone rings.)*

GRENDALL: Look at the Bloomburg. See what wireless is doing?

EDDIE: Wo.

MARIE: *(On her phone)* Hey! It's you! It's Him! It's you! Hey, you!

GRENDALL: Every time the man names a sector, the sector starts acting like her.

MARIE: Sure, we're watching! You're amazing! Are you coming back soon?

EDDIE: *(Quietly, with a nod at* MARIE*)* So who is she?

GRENDALL: That's the new "niece."

EDDIE: The new niece?

GRENDALL: I take a trip, maybe I bring back a case of wine. He brings those.

EDDIE: She seems nice.

GRENDALL: Right. According to rumor?

EDDIE: Uh huh?

GRENDALL: She's the Heart Attack.

EDDIE: Get out.

GRENDALL: With Him When It Hit.

EDDIE: Wo. But you said you and she—?

GRENDALL: I've called dibs on next game, know what I'm saying?

EDDIE: Loud and clear.

(Lights back up on TORIA *and* BELMONT*)*

TORIA: I'm Toria Bruno, back with Gus Belmont, the most sought-after genius on Wall Street. You are picking...

BELMONT: Wireless.

TORIA: Why? What does your market analysis show you?

BELMONT: I'll tell you. I was sitting in an airport yesterday, and an idea came to me. In the form of a young business traveler.

EDDIE: Oh my God.

BELMONT: We started talking about wireless, which as you know is the future of all communication.

EDDIE: That was me. Oh my God.

BELMONT: And maybe that's all genius really is. You get known as an open person, and this world constantly offers to lead you into the future. Which is wireless. And that's all I'm going to say right now.

TORIA: Outstanding. This is Toria Bruno saying, watch what happens.

(Lights out on BELMONT *and* TORIA*)*

EDDIE: That was me! Leading him into the future? That's what Gus Belmont thinks of my piece of sheetcake, okay? What he was saying, that was me!

GRENDALL: I guess I owe you an apology.

EDDIE: Okay.

GRENDALL: So. The...Gizmo? Nice. Retro.

EDDIE: Thanks.

GRENDALL: How did this all come about?

EDDIE: Well. I got an idea.

GRENDALL: How sweet the sound.

EDDIE: I looked over the market and I said, put this over here with this way over here and—

GRENDALL: And it's a bouncing baby idea.

EDDIE: I hired a couple of kids to do the coding.

GRENDALL: Who owns the code?

EDDIE: I own the code.

GRENDALL: You're sure.

EDDIE: I am sure. It was my idea.

GRENDALL: Forgive my asking, you'd be amazed, at the very beginning, a simple little question.

EDDIE: Sure. And I was skipping, but if you want to take all the steps I had done the market analysis.

GRENDALL: Is there a preexisting identified market?

EDDIE: Not yet.

MARIE: Well, that can't be good. Can it? *(Off their look)* Sorry.

GRENDALL: So, here you are, still.

MARIE: Can I be here with you guys? Just till Himself gets back? Plus because when we were on the phone just now he asked what I was up to and I said I was in the room where you two guys were meeting and he said great let him know how it goes. So. Can I?

(Beat)

EDDIE: No problem for me.

GRENDALL: Well. Just another example of our unstructured, freewheeling, brainstormin' ways here at Prospera.

EDDIE: *(To* MARIE*)* See, if there's a previously identified market—

MARIE: Uh huh—

EDDIE: —somebody else can identify it, too—

MARIE: Gotcha! Okay, but then—

GRENDALL: So where did you get this idea?

(Beat)

EDDIE: I said.

GRENDALL: No. You said you got an idea, but you didn't say from where.

EDDIE: Where do people get ideas? They notice a need.

GRENDALL: How?

EDDIE: I heard some guys talking at a party. Complaining about how they could never get their personal digital things to do what they really wanted. And they said—

GRENDALL: They said, hey, you're a businessy kind of guy, we've had an idea for a company, listen to this. And you said—

EDDIE: It wasn't like that. Why does this matter?

GRENDALL: Because you weren't shaving when you got this idea, or driving along singing a song, you weren't even messing around with your own personal digital thingy when you got this idea. You got it from other people.

EDDIE: With other people.

GRENDALL: Why aren't they here?

EDDIE: They were guys at a party, how do I—

GRENDALL: Were they the guys you bought the code from? *(Beat)* Sure they were. So when you say you got this idea what you mean is that you bought this idea. So you could walk in here like Young Tom Edison. Right? *(Beat)* You did buy the code.

EDDIE: Outright. Absolutely. Contracts signed, all rights waived. One's in Albuquerque, one's in Florida somewhere.

GRENDALL: They'll be back if this hits. With lawyers.

MARIE: And he's right. It messes up the story.

EDDIE: I had been thinking about this problem myself. That's why I pursued the conversation.

GRENDALL: Sure.

EDDIE: Anybody can have an idea. It takes an entrepreneur to bring it to market.

GRENDALL: So, we could bring it to market. What do we need you for?

EDDIE: Hey.

GRENDALL: We were talking with a guy, and we had an idea. We paid him off and we brought it to market.

EDDIE: You can't do that.

GRENDALL: Why not? You did.

EDDIE: Try it. You are not the only ones I've told this to. There's a trail. People know.

GRENDALL: And here I thought you came to us first.

EDDIE: Nobody comes to you first! Because of shit like this! I have lived with this idea for two years. I have grown it. It is mine now. I was the one who pulled it together, made it a design, hammered out a product description. I paid everybody. I maxed my cards. Because I saw this picture. People every morning, putting in their pockets their wallet, their keys, and something I made. The Gizmo. I staked everything. I am maxed out.

(Fast forward. BELMONT *enters, clapping. Same people, same room, different time)*

BELMONT: Excellent presentation, son. Now, I'm no technician. The technicians are going over this with a fine-toothed comb. But you're talking about a single computing platform compatible with every kind of wireless data transfer. A single standard. You're talking about getting everybody to sign up for a single standard.

EDDIE: That's right.

BELMONT: Tall order.

EDDIE: That's why I came to you. Tall orders is what you do.

BELMONT: You see that? Confidence. You see that, Grendall?

GRENDALL: Yes.

EDDIE: With you behind me, sir, there is nothing I can't do. I honestly believe that.

BELMONT: Belief. That's what you need. The capacity for belief.

EDDIE: I am about total dedication. I have a five-year plan. I am about nothing but making this company succeed. I am not breathing till I'm thirty.

BELMONT: What if something happens?

EDDIE: Lot of things are going to happen, I'm making things happen.

BELMONT: What if the market changes?

EDDIE: I'm assuming the market's going to change. Change is in the paradigm.

BELMONT: What if something changes your priorities?

EDDIE: Not going to happen. My priorities are marketproof.

BELMONT: Jeez, did I used to be like this?

MARIE: You must have been, or you wouldn't be where you are now.

BELMONT: To get to me you have to start with that?

MARIE: You don't remember?

BELMONT: It was a different time. Understand, my generation was at the forefront of changes unknown to human history.

MARIE: Everybody says that.

BELMONT: I had hair down to here.

MARIE: *(Flipping through the magazine with* BELMONT's *face on the cover)* I thought you were a trainee at I B M.

BELMONT: What?

MARIE: You must have worn a blue suit right through the revolution.

BELMONT: There was a commune, upstate New York, everybody working together in common. It was beautiful.

MARIE: I B M. He's talking about I B M.

BELMONT: Silks we wore. Colors so bright. Paisleys and polka dots. We worked in silks.

MARIE: He's talking about the neckties. Blue suit, white shirt, the one spot of color, that's what you remember.

BELMONT: Then I got into this whole Eastern philosophy thing.

MARIE: The Japanese, in the '80s, in that bank, you were studying Japanese corporations. I wish you wouldn't go on television, Gus, it messes with your head.

*(*BELMONT *looks at* MARIE. *Beat)*

BELMONT: Grendall? See me?

*(*BELMONT *and* GRENDALL *exit.)*

MARIE: Sorry sorry sorry... *(Beat; to* EDDIE*)* I hope you don't mind he let me watch—

EDDIE: No, no.

MARIE: I thought he'd like that I'm interested. But I must be doing something right, huh? Can't believe I'm still here.

EDDIE: I know what you mean.

MARIE: Oh, you did great, I could tell. Listen, could I ask a stupid question if you promise not to tell?

EDDIE: You really are interested.

MARIE: How couldn't I be? Beats what I was doing.

EDDIE: What's that?

MARIE: I was hanging out, auditing classes?

EDDIE: In what?

MARIE: Comparative religion, cultural anthropology?

EDDIE: Where, around here?

MARIE: The Sorbonne?

EDDIE: Wo.

MARIE: Nothing to wo about, you get so many lames at the Sorbonne? Taking drugs and dancing like monkeys. Tonight they're gonna party like it's 1929. They don't see it coming.

EDDIE: See what?

MARIE: Okay, thank God, this is what I've been dying to ask somebody, because here's what I don't get. 1929.

EDDIE: The Stock Market Crash?

MARIE: Right. You've studied this stuff. Doesn't all this here seem kind of...familiar?

EDDIE: You don't think we're in a similar situation.

MARIE: Well, there's the wide-spread stock speculation, heavy margin buying, rampant overpricing, a weakened banking system, a massive bubble effect brought on by overexcitement over new technology issues, early signs of major startup washout, too much money chasing too few good investments, those are the only similarities I can see.

EDDIE: Well, that may be true, but the Internet has totally changed the rules of sound investment.

MARIE: Okay, but see, if you delete "Internet," and insert "Radio and the Autombile," you just quoted your great-grandpa.

EDDIE: No kidding.

MARIE: I've gotta keep on this, 'cause everyone gets it but me.

(MARIE *and* EDDIE *exit as* BELMONT *and* GRENDALL *enter.* BELMONT'*s office*)

BELMONT: Now. This one.

GRENDALL: You think?

BELMONT: We've got a fund maker here.

GRENDALL: Oh for—based on what?

BELMONT: This is what I tried to tell you, Grendall, back in your startup days. People need to see that light around you.

GRENDALL: Absolutely.

BELMONT: That aura.

GRENDALL: Right.

BELMONT: That's the thing you don't see around the guys who are going to crater their startups.

GRENDALL: And you see it clearly here.

BELMONT: I'm not blind. Who couldn't see that?

GRENDALL: Is there anything I should know?

BELMONT: You do put a lot of faith in knowledge, Grendall.

GRENDALL: So do you. Best due diligence in the business.

BELMONT: I was scared for a long time. Second-guessing myself. Wasted years of my life.

GRENDALL: The years you were making your first billion dollars? These are the wasted years we're talking about?

BELMONT: When I think of what I could have done if I'd trusted myself. But now I know what I'm doing. You'll run this, won't you? Handle the C E O stuff? Keep Fisker free to be the media mascot?

GRENDALL: Me?

BELMONT: You've got other plans?

GRENDALL: I'm working on several—

BELMONT: Can't lounge around forever. Get a job, Carbo.

GRENDALL: I'm just a few weeks away from—

BELMONT: Do this in the meantime.

GRENDALL: Running this—we're talking about three years, five—

BELMONT: Oh, no, no. Year, year and a half at the most. Talk to legal, see how fast we can let your options vest.

GRENDALL: You want me to build this guy a company?

BELMONT: Money a-raising, work a-doing, customers a-buying. I'll do the rest.

GRENDALL: Can I outsource some things?

BELMONT: Outsource everything, that's the only way this works. We'll get you a list of vendors.

GRENDALL: It would help if I had some idea what was going on.

BELMONT: Business as usual, Carbo.

GRENDALL: At three times the usual pace.

BELMONT: Like I said, business as usual. And you'll walk away with enough to do whatever you want.

GRENDALL: I want to have my youth back.

BELMONT: Plenty of time for that later. Look at me.

(BELMONT *exits. Quick fast forward.* EDDIE *enters.*)

EDDIE: Is he going to fund me? Am I funded? What? What are you looking at?

GRENDALL: I don't know.

EDDIE: Have you heard anything? What do you think?

GRENDALL: I think...

(GRENDALL *points the remote. Lights up on* TORIA)

GRENDALL: Yes.

TORIA: Word on the Street says Gus Belmont of Propera Funds has funded first-tier financing for a major new startup in the super-hot wireless communications sector.

EDDIE: That's me! That's me!

TORIA: Through a spokesman, Gus Belmont says, "We're doing financing rounds so fast on this thing they're going to rear-end each other. We're starting a whole new fund. Prospera number Five—

EDDIE: A new fund? Wo!

TORIA: "—with this startup, the Gizmo, as the hook."

GRENDALL: We can switch it off—

TORIA: And rumor has it that Gus Belmont is raising Carbury Grendall from the dead and putting him in charge of this hot new startup! If at first you don't succeed—

GRENDALL: *(Pointing the remote)* —eat shit and die.

(Lights out on TORIA*)*

EDDIE: Yes! Yes! I'm funded! I am funded! *(Kissing* GRENDALL *full on the mouth)* Yes!

GRENDALL: Congratulations.

EDDIE: Thank you!

GRENDALL: Don't ever touch me again.

EDDIE: Hey. We don't have a contract yet.

GRENDALL: Details.

EDDIE: We haven't worked out the terms—I haven't agreed to any terms—

GRENDALL: Right, we'll have to do that. Because we might not be able to come to terms and you might walk away. *(Bursts out laughing, stops)* Sorry.

EDDIE: I might.

GRENDALL: Look, this is how he works. He makes up his mind, it's all over the world, and reality is a detail for the peons to clean up.

EDDIE: I am funded. *(Frantically thumb-typing his two-way pager)* I Am Funded! Sending to...Everybody!

GRENDALL: Do you know what he put me through when I came to him? Vetting my credentials, crunching, recrunching my numbers, umpteen presentations just to pry loose a lousy two million and I had to do my own heavy lifting, I didn't have me to help me.

EDDIE: Are you sure you want to do this?

GRENDALL: Absolutely. I am one thousand percent behind this idea and I'm thrilled to be a part of it.

EDDIE: I'm glad to hear that, because you know I have been about this idea—

GRENDALL: I believe you! Now I've got to interview guys who can be director of business development for our little lemonade stand and raise this massive new fund at the same time—

EDDIE: A new fund. Wo.

GRENDALL: And you need to be all about marketing.

EDDIE: Not design and manufacturing? Product test?

(TOM *enters.*)

TOM: Oh, manufacturing *is* marketing for guys like you. It's all marketing, janitorial is marketing now. You're not in high tech, you're in show biz.

GRENDALL: Amen. I'm Carbury Grendall.

TOM: I've heard about you, hi, I'm Tom.

GRENDALL: Whatever you heard, I did not crater my startup.

TOM: Nah, I know some guys you went to Wharton with.

GRENDALL: Really, who?

TOM: Don't sweat it, the story dies with me. And you must be The Kid With the Gizmo!

EDDIE: Nice to meet you, Tom...?

(MARIE *enters.*)

MARIE: Have you guys seen Himself?

GRENDALL: Not since this morning, is he—

EDDIE: Hey, Marie.

MARIE: Hey, Eddie.

TOM: Marie? I think we've met, hi, I'm Tom?

MARIE: Hi. Tom what?

TOM: You were in Switzerland with my sister Carol?

MARIE: Carol? Ohhh. Oh God. So you're Tom.

TOM: Hi. Jeez, huh?

MARIE: Carol talked about you all the time. I was so sorry when I heard about her.

TOM: Thanks. You look great.

MARIE: I was lucky.

(BELMONT *enters.*)

BELMONT: I'm going to have to run in a second—

MARIE: There you are, the plane's waiting—

BELMONT: Just wanted to stick my head in. Hiya, son.

TOM: This is great. I didn't think I'd get an audience with the Pope, you know? I'm honored and all.

BELMONT: Children, you are looking at one of the great family dynasties in twentieth century industry. Knocking on my door.

TOM: Guys. Hi. Tom Xerox.

EDDIE: Uh, hi. Wo.

TOM: You look like you're all over your heart thing.

BELMONT: Kind of you. How's your grandfather?

TOM: Fine I guess.

BELMONT: I'm surprised the family sent you out on this. I didn't know they'd passed this kind of thing on to you.

TOM: Sorry, I'm not following.

GRENDALL: No, Mr Belmont, Tom here is—

BELMONT: We're only interested in a few large-scale investors, if they're not going to take this seriously—

TOM: Oh, no, the family's not looking to invest.

BELMONT: No?

TOM: Well, maybe they are, I don't know, you'd want to be talking to my uncles about that, I guess.

BELMONT: Now I'm not following. Why are you here?

GRENDALL: We heard about Tom from—

TOM: Sir, I'm here about a job.

BELMONT: Is that right. Say now.

GRENDALL: Tom has quite an intriguing resume.

TOM: I do? Neat.

BELMONT: I'll leave you to it, then.

MARIE: Bye.

(BELMONT *and* MARIE *exit.*)

GRENDALL: Thanks for dropping by, sir—

EDDIE: One question.

TOM: Sure.

EDDIE: You can't need the money.

TOM: God, no.

GRENDALL: No, given his family, I don't think he needs the money.

TOM: No, given my family, I need another family. Kidding.

EDDIE: We're demanding a lot out of people. We're putting this together really fast. None of us really has what you'd call a life right now.

TOM: Sounds good. How much money am I raising?

GRENDALL: More than enough. Belmont said to raise more than enough.

EDDIE: Wait. Won't that dilute everyone's equity share?

GRENDALL: Get out of the box.

EDDIE: I don't follow.

GRENDALL: Don't try to follow. Just keep up.

(As the guys exit, lights up on BELMONT, *staring outward, pointing and clicking.* MARIE *enters, carrying a tray full of pill bottles.)*

MARIE: Hey. It's that time.

BELMONT: I have to do this.

MARIE: You need to take your medication.

BELMONT: I've got an interview, we're bombing Yugoslavia, they need to know what I think.

MARIE: What do you think about Yugoslavia?

BELMONT: That's why I can't do that now, I have to figure out what I think about Yugoslavia!

MARIE: Should you give opinion-maker interviews about things you have no opinion about?

BELMONT: The market needs to know what to think. Who are they supposed to believe, some politician?

MARIE: Someone who knows any facts about the situation?

BELMONT: I used to believe in Adam Smith's Invisible Hand, that it was all mass movement, I was wrong, I see it now. The herd follows where it's led.

MARIE: Oh for—and that's you? The Good Shepherd?

BELMONT: I say it and it happens! Don't you see what an opportunity that is?

MARIE: You are not creating the world by speaking it! Take your medication!

BELMONT: Not now.

MARIE: It's not a snack bar. You have to take all of them, on a schedule, or you will wreck yourself.

BELMONT: Get out, stop distracting me.

MARIE: Listen—

BELMONT: Stop distracting me! We will all fall to pieces if you distract me!

MARIE: Why am I here? Why do you want me here? You are a human being, not a market force.

BELMONT: Of course I'm a human being. Of course I'm a market force. I used to read the markets. But now... I've crossed over, somehow. I'm not reading it anymore. I'm writing it. There is a music to it and nobody hears it but me. Up, down, slow, fast. Buy hold sell. How could I know that if I hadn't written it myself? Answer me that.

MARIE: I can't.

BELMONT: Of course you can't. It's just logical. It's not me. It's just logic.

MARIE: But aren't the markets getting all jittery or something?

BELMONT: Vertigo, that's all. New heights every day. People get disoriented.

MARIE: Not you, though.

BELMONT: Pretty soon, I'll be so big they won't make a move for fear if it hurts me it hurts everyone. I'm almost part of the organism. And then.

MARIE: Then?

BELMONT: Then I can start making something out of nothing. Make it rise and walk. You just watch this Gizmo thing, you'll see what I mean. Don't you sell me short. (*He exits.*)

MARIE: Oh I'm not.

(MARIE *sits and looks outward at what* BELMONT *was seeing. Lights up on* TORIA)

TORIA: Toria Bruno, and today's Word on the Street is "selling short." For those of you new to investing, and gosh! there's a bunch of you this year, short selling is investing spelled backwards. Instead of buying a stock and hoping the price goes up, you're betting that the price will go down! Here's how it works: *(Fast)* You borrow a stock through your broker and sell it right away, for delivery at a later date, gambling that by delivery time, the price will have dropped, so you can buy it for less than your agreed-upon selling price, replace the shares you borrowed, sold and just delivered with the cheaper shares you just bought, and keep the difference as your profit. But if the price goes up, not down, who has to pony up the difference? You, Mister Short! Confused? Of course you are!

(Lights out on TORIA *and up on* GRENDALL, EDDIE, *and* TOM, *with luggage, on phones. They are in various airports.* MARIE *is still in* BELMONT'*s office.)*

GRENDALL: Carbury Grendall for Mister Belmont.

TOM: Tom Xerox.

EDDIE: Eddie Fisker, there's a conference call?

TOM: Tom Xerox. Can people hear me?

MARIE: Hi, it's Marie.

EDDIE: It's Eddie!

TOM: Hey, Eddie! EntreBoy!

EDDIE: Nice to have you back! How was Europe?

MARIE: Bunch of lames, I missed you boys.

GRENDALL: You're answering the phones now?

MARIE: I asked him if I could sit in.

EDDIE: Listen, we need to start, I've got a plane.

TOM: Me too.

GRENDALL: We're supposed to be checking in with Himself about our company-building process. Where is he?

MARIE: He needed to deal with some things. I'm sitting in.

GRENDALL: You're—you're—is his mobile on, do you know?

MARIE: Try it. This is his idea, though.

GRENDALL: He—why didn't he tell me himself?

MARIE: Didn't he? I thought he was. He sounded like he was.

EDDIE: He probably would have told us today.

TOM: Sure.

EDDIE: If he'd been here.

GRENDALL: I don't like to think we're being downgraded.

EDDIE: Get out of the box, Grendall.

GRENDALL: We need to start, where's Tom?

TOM: I'm here.

EDDIE: Should we start without him, you think?

TOM: *I'm here!*

MARIE: Hey, Tom!

GRENDALL: Bad connection.

TOM: *(Perching awkwardly on the lip of the stage)* Can you hear me now?

MARIE: Loud and clear, Tom. Where are you?

TOM: Don't know, too tired, I'll check my Palm.

EDDIE: Any day now, we'll all be saying—

ALL: I'll check with my Gizmo!

TOM: There are lobsters in the gift shops.

EDDIE: What are they buying?

TOM: For sale, doofus.

GRENDALL: You're in Maine, Tom!

EDDIE: He's in San Francisco!

TOM: There's a lot of plaid products in the gift shops.

GRENDALL: Portland! You're in Portland!

EDDIE: Portland, Maine or Portland, Oregon?

GRENDALL: This could go either way. Are they Pendleton or L L Bean?

TOM: Bean.

GRENDALL: You're in Portland, Maine, Tom!

TOM: Ding ding ding!

EDDIE: Could have found out faster with a Gizmo.

GRENDALL: Patience, patience.

MARIE: Where are you, Eddie?

EDDIE: Meeting the place who gave the low bid for manufacturing. Where are you, Carbo?

GRENDALL: Meeting a couple of places who want to be our finance department.

EDDIE: Hey, are we going to hire some people?

GRENDALL: Nah, I'll contract it out.

EDDIE: Outsourcing.

GRENDALL: Absolutely. And I don't know when I'm back, I've got to meet one of the places bidding for the human resources contract.

EDDIE: You're outsourcing the human resources department?

GRENDALL: Sure.

EDDIE: Why do we need a human resources department? We've got no employees!

GRENDALL: Can't have a good-looking firm without a human resources department. I am outsourcing everything. I would outsource my own bodily functions if I could. Look, it's Himself's idea.

TOM: A Virtual Company. The man is a genius.

GRENDALL: Got that right.

EDDIE: Yup. Yup yup yup.

GRENDALL: They're a good company, they're in our *keiretsu*.

EDDIE: So's the place I am, they're in our *keiretsu* too.

TOM: Belmont must have his finger everywhere.

(Freeze. Lights up on TORIA*)*

TORIA: Toria Bruno, and today's Word on the Street is *keiretsu*, pronounced: kay *ret* soo, from the Japanese meaning a bunch of companies with interlocking directorships and contractual relationships and frankly a kind of fortress mentality, I'm sorry, it just seems sneaky to me.

*(*BELMONT *enters, clapping. The conference room. Everybody gathers.)*

BELMONT: Hell of a demo, son! Got to take my hat off to you.

EDDIE: Thank you. Credit to the guys in design, they're really earning their stock options.

BELMONT: They're not earning much else, though, are they?

GRENDALL: No, no, very little outflow that way.

EDDIE: So what's the next step? When do we start making these?

BELMONT: Well, you should definitely make the big announcement.

GRENDALL: Absolutely.

TOM: The market's gonna eat this up.

EDDIE: Good, so, then, manufacturing, actually making them...

BELMONT: First things first. You know, we could see you rolling out a whole series of announcements.

GRENDALL: I've been pleased with the people we contracted the P R to.

BELMONT: Yes, that's been a good acquisition.

EDDIE: They're one of yours?

BELMONT: Oh yes.

EDDIE: Huh. So you're paying yourself. Basically.

BELMONT: The people who are investing in your fine company are paying the people who invested in that other fine company, and we all look productive and the market stays happy and continues to invest.

EDDIE: I'm sorry, I thought we were going to start making my Gizmos. But what we're going to make is announcements.

BELMONT: What we are going to make, son, is money. We are selling potential and when you're selling that, the whole blue sky is the limit. As soon as you start selling products, you're a sitting duck. Enjoy this time, son, you'll never be this free again. We'll look to see a presentation on those announcements on Monday. *(He exits.)*

TOM: The man is a genius.

EDDIE: Yup. Yup yup yup.

MARIE: Guys? He's talking about creating a need, okay? By the time this comes to market, he wants it to be the hottest new product of the year. We want them to be aching for it. So we've got to tease them first, we've got to flirt, show a little at a time. We're going to get a reputation. We want them fantasizing how it'll change their lives. They'll be wanting it so bad. First the young ones, the ones who are up for anything. Then the older ones, they'll feel if they don't leave their old ways of doing things for us, they'll barely be men anymore. If we play this right, they're going to marry this technology before we have to put out a thing. And then. Well. Hey, excuse me, guys. It's that time. *(She exits.)*

GRENDALL: I feel violated.

TOM: Me too. Though not in a bad way.

(Lights up on EDDIE, *as cameras flash. As he speaks, lights up on* GRENDALL, *poised over his laptop, and elsewhere,* MARIE, *both watching* EDDIE *on T V)*

EDDIE: *(Working hard)* I know that, uh, usually, at a product launch, you expect to actually see a...product. But, the uh, the point is, the Gizmo, the physical *(Cupping his hand around nothing)* Gizmo, is only part of the picture.

GRENDALL: *(On the phone)* For Christ's sake, somebody get the kid a prop!

EDDIE: We need the corporate culture and the consumer universe to believe in the standard, the single—so, our strategy, and this, this is classic Gus Belmont, we're going to go public first, really get the market invested in this idea. Five years from now, we'll have trouble remembering a time when the Gizmo *(Again the handful of nothing)* didn't exist. Those of us, all of us at Gizmo, we feel like that already, like, hasn't this always been here? Even though it doesn't literally, you know, exist, at all, yet. Gizmo.

(Lights down on EDDIE*)*

MARIE: *(On the phone)* Carbo—

GRENDALL: *(On the phone)* I'll be riiight with you.

MARIE: Jesus Christ, I was just—I'd never taken the public elevator, I was riding up, the door opened... There's a whole other floor down there.

GRENDALL: Oh, you found the Engine Room.

MARIE: They're staring into space, or they're screaming at each other, and the lights—the fluorescents that make your skin look dead—they look like hell. What are they?

GRENDALL: Stock brokers. Securities traders, currencies, sector analysts—

MARIE: They're part of Prospera?

GRENDALL: When Belmont makes a decision—go long in oil futures, force the devaluation of the peso— somebody has to carry it out.

MARIE: Oh my God. They're the Oompa-Loompas. Himself is Willy Wonka, he has all these Oompa-Loompas. So they're down there, like, day-trading?

GRENDALL: In everything. On a very, very, very large scale.

MARIE: Like what you're doing right now, only bigger?

GRENDALL: *(Shutting the laptop)* No. Me? Day trading? No.

MARIE: Aren't you supposed to do that on personal time?

GRENDALL: Personal time? Personal time. What, like after I retire?

MARIE: No, like, when you're done working for the day.

GRENDALL: Honey, it's three a.m. here, we're not even having this conversation.

(Beep. EDDIE *enters, on the phone, whipped.)*

GRENDALL: You want to take that?

MARIE: That's okay.

GRENDALL: I'll be done with my business day when my business days are done. And that is never going to happen, because I do not have a Fuck You Fund.

MARIE: A which?

GRENDALL: A Fuck You Fund, the guys that say "fuck you all!" and walk away, all those guys have leveraged their stock in their non-cratered startups into a diversified portfolio and a big fat goddamn boat and a woman like you.

(Beat. MARIE *and* GRENDALL *do not hear:)*

EDDIE: Hey, Marie, it's Eddie, Eddie Fisker, you remember, with the Gizmo?

GRENDALL: So they can sail off into the sunset screaming "fuck you all!"

MARIE: Do you have a boat?

GRENDALL: If I had a boat I'd be on a boat, do I sound like I'm on a boat?

MARIE: How do people sound when they're on a boat?

GRENDALL: They sound like this: *(As he pulls the phone away from his face)* Fuck...you...aaalll...

(Lights down on GRENDALL, *up on* TOM, *with a mike and an easel. A conference room in a big corporate headquarters)*

TOM: Gentlemen...and Ms. This is the sweetest sight in the world to me: a room full of managers in their forties and fifties, or as I like to call it, Jurassic Park. Yesterday you thought you were hot 'cause you figured out how to read your email. This morning you got an email from the president saying you need to have an Internet plan. Mmm. Smell the fear. Too young for early retirement and way too old to get this shit. Well, fellas...and fellette. I have an Internet plan. "Wait a second, Tom Xerox has an Internet plan? I watched him grow up in *People* magazine, he's a friggin' idiot, he's got an Internet plan?" Yeah, I do. My Internet plan is: Eddie Fisker. The Kid With the Gizmo. The guy who will not rest until everyone on this planet is connected to everyone else. It's a new world. And here's how I know. My name is Tom Xerox. And this year I went to work for Eddie Fisker.

(Lights up on EDDIE, *on the phone)*

EDDIE: And this works?

TOM: *(On the phone)* I have here an order for ten thousand Gizmos.

EDDIE: They're okay that what they're buying doesn't exist yet?

TOM: They've been up all night trying to read *Wired* magazine with their bifocals, all they know is, if it already exists, they're not supposed to want it. Oh, and I tell them "Change is in the paradigm." They love that shit.

EDDIE: They love that, huh? Change is in the paradigm. They *get* that.

TOM: Kid, they don't know what paradigm means.
They don't know how to spell paradigm.

EDDIE: So what do all these people think they're buying?

TOM: EntreBoy. *I* don't know what they're buying.
Do I know how a Gizmo works? I'm selling you.

EDDIE: What about the fundamentals, they don't care?

TOM: Fundamentals? Here's the fundamentals.
They know me. I know you. You know Belmont.
And we all want a piece of what Belmont's got.
That's the fundamentals.

EDDIE: Tom, do you ever think that things aren't
what they seem?

TOM: Boy, I'm a salesman. Things are *only* what they
seem.

(MARIE *joins* EDDIE, *carrying a book.*)

MARIE: Hey.

EDDIE: Tom. Later.

(EDDIE *hangs up. Lights out on* TOM)

MARIE: You're here.

EDDIE: Yeah, sorry.

MARIE: Don't apologize.

EDDIE: No, it's just, when I'm on the road, I'm a profit
center. If I'm sitting here I'm a cost center.

MARIE: You sound like Carbo.

EDDIE: You're saying that like it's a bad thing.

MARIE: One of him is enough.

EDDIE: Interesting. Where's Himself?

MARIE: Sleeping. I hope he is. I'll git.

EDDIE: Park it here if you like.

MARIE: You're working.

EDDIE: Just replying to three hundred E-mails.
What's that?

MARIE: A book?

EDDIE: Little paper websites, I remember these.
I know it's a book, schnook, what book?

MARIE: *Crossing the Chasm.*

EDDIE: What a great book! You're reading that book?
I love that book!

MARIE: It's about technology marketing.

EDDIE: Yeah! You want some tea? I think there's
something herbal around here.

MARIE: Got anything stronger?

EDDIE: Interesting.

MARIE: Like with caffeine.

EDDIE: Oddly even more interesting. *(He exits.)*

MARIE: Thanks. You sure I'm not—

EDDIE: *(Calling from off)* Believe me, I'm used to working
with people around. I'm used to working anywhere.
Thank You, Amazing Technology— *(A fan hums, off.
He enters.)* And that's nothing. When everybody has a
Gizmo—

MARIE: You don't have to sell me.

EDDIE: I'm not. I'm like this all the time.

MARIE: You can't be. You'd die.

EDDIE: Why?

MARIE: Somebody would kill you. Do you ever wonder
what's going to happen to you?

EDDIE: When?

MARIE: After the thing that's going to happen. There's a Gizmo in every pot, you're a public company—that's the plan, right?

EDDIE: That's *my* plan.

MARIE: Then what?

EDDIE: Then? Man. Build better Gizmos.

MARIE: But after you've...succeeded. What about you?

EDDIE: Me? Man. After? I'll be a totally different person. Some rich, successful guy. I don't know. That guy's a stranger to me. I'm not going to make his plans for him.

MARIE: You sound like you really resent him.

EDDIE: Who?

MARIE: FutureYou. You sound like you hate him.

EDDIE: Well, I'm working like a dog for the guy. And I hate working for somebody else.

MARIE: So you're busting your butt to become something you hate. Sure, okay.

EDDIE: Big smug jerk, looking down on sweaty little scum like me. He'd just better be grateful, that's all. Why do you ask?

MARIE: I don't know. You're a natural energy resource. You'd be a shame to waste.

EDDIE: You're sweet.

MARIE: Ha.

EDDIE: You are.

MARIE: How did you get so normal?

EDDIE: What, I had a middle-class upbringing—

MARIE: That must be it.

EDDIE: My folks stayed together for most of my childhood.

MARIE: You luckout.

EDDIE: Come on, you went to boarding school in Switzerland with Tom Xerox's sister, how rough is that?

MARIE: Boarding school? Is that what you think it was?

EDDIE: You, Carol, I hear rich teenage girls, I hear Switzerland, I think boarding school. No?

MARIE: Oh my God. Do you *have* a dark side?

EDDIE: Oh, when guys think about girls in boarding school, there's definitely a dark side.

MARIE: Even your kinks are normal.

EDDIE: Switzerland, what else, cuckoo clocks?

MARIE: You're half right.

EDDIE: The...clock half?

MARIE: The other half.

EDDIE: Oh. Wo.

(Beat. A bell dings, off. EDDIE *exits.* MARIE *sits in silence.* EDDIE *enters, carrying mugs. He hands one to* MARIE.*)*

EDDIE: Here you go.

MARIE: Thanks.

(He sits at his laptop. She holds her book.)

MARIE: This is nice.

EDDIE: Yeah, like I said, that's the deal with this stuff, you can work anywhere, any circumstances. Work from home.

MARIE: You're not working from home.

EDDIE: Sure I am. Here we are in the den.

MARIE: Oh, yeah. Cozy.

EDDIE: Come on, work with me. I've got my paperwork to catch up on, there's nothing on the tube, you've got a good book to curl up with, come keep me company. Are you cold?

MARIE: The tea hits the spot.

EDDIE: If you get cold, there's that blanket my mother crocheted for me, wrap it round you.

MARIE: Where?

EDDIE: Work with me. It's there on the back of the sofa.

MARIE: What sofa, there's no—

EDDIE: Work with me.

MARIE: Oh. Gotcha.

EDDIE: I could build a fire if you want.

MARIE: In the...fireplace?

EDDIE: Correct.

MARIE: That's too much trouble, I'm fine.

EDDIE: You're sure? Maybe later.

MARIE: This is cozy, just like this. Sipping my tea. From the souvenir mugs we got when we went to that place that time.

EDDIE: Outstanding.

MARIE: Boy, you're right. This is some amazing technology.

(BELMONT, GRENDALL, and TOM enter. GRENDALL is holding a pitch book.)

BELMONT: Outstanding work. People, we are ready for the Road Show.

EDDIE: We...are?

(Freeze. Lights up on TORIA*)*

TORIA: The Road Show. Meeting hundreds of fund managers and institutional investors in dozens of cities in fourteen days to say, "High tech lets people work anywhere. That's what we flew here to tell you. Isn't it ironic? Buy our stock anyhow."

(Lights out on TORIA*)*

BELMONT: Oh, all the ducks are in a row, aren't they, Grendall?

GRENDALL: Absolutely.

EDDIE: They are?

GRENDALL: Absolutely.

EDDIE: So we're going to start talking to places about brokering the initial public offering?

BELMONT: Done.

EDDIE: Really?

BELMONT: Give it to him, Grendall.

*(*GRENDALL *hands* EDDIE *a pitch book.)*

EDDIE: *(Moved, quietly)* Wo.

MARIE: What is that?

TOM: It's kind of a sales brochure for the company. We call it a pitch book.

MARIE: But that's not our logo on the cover.

TOM: It's the logo of the brokerage company that'll be handling the stock.

EDDIE: J P Morgan.

BELMONT: They were eager for the business. And I thought the Gizmo would look good in a Morgan cover.

EDDIE: Mr Belmont...

BELMONT: Happy Birthday, son.

MARIE: Eddie! Is it your birthday?

EDDIE: I guess it is now.

TOM: The market is going to love you guys.

MARIE: They're going to love the Gizmo.

GRENDALL: Hey. Yes. Very effective.

TOM: It's like we're making everyone an imaginary friend.

EDDIE: Kind of.

TOM: Did you have one of those?

GRENDALL: What other kind do you need?

MARIE: I don't remember.

BELMONT: I had so many.

EDDIE: You did, sir?

BELMONT: Thousands of them. I'd see them everywhere.

MARIE: Hey, it's that time.

GRENDALL: Having a bonding moment here—imaginary friends, what, other kids? Animals?

TOM: Investors of the future?

MARIE: We really need to—

BELMONT: Oh, no. Thrones, dominions, seraphim, dancing. And the saints, of course. Everyone's guardian angel. The world was thick with them.

EDDIE: You must have been a very religious boy, thinking about that stuff all the time.

BELMONT: No, no. I thought I was God. Isn't that something?

(Beat)

EDDIE: That's hilarious.

GRENDALL: Really? God?

BELMONT: Creator and judge of the universe. Oh, yes.

GRENDALL: That's hysterical.

BELMONT: Is it? It was a very scary thought for a boy to carry around. What if I told someone, and the devil found out, and came for me and killed me? What would happen to the world, if I died?

EDDIE: You're right, that's quite the little fantasy life. When did you grow out of it?

TOM: Therapy? Therapy does wonders.

BELMONT: Never touched the stuff. They might have put me away, and then where would the world be?

EDDIE: Adolescence, did that take care of it? Girls had a way of making me feel barely even human, much less—

BELMONT: No. Oh, no, I had to keep quiet about it for years.

TOM: What finally happened?

BELMONT: I became incredibly wealthy, and governments and markets all over the world are made and unmade by a single word from me.

EDDIE: Oh.

GRENDALL: You're living the dream then.

BELMONT: I'm contented. I feel I've been accepted for myself. *(He exits.)*

GRENDALL: Well. Back to work.

TOM: Look at my call sheet.

MARIE: See ya.

EDDIE: Wait a second!

GRENDALL: I'm sorry, I thought we were done.

EDDIE: He thinks he's God?

MARIE: He must be really comfortable with you guys. He hardly ever talks about his childhood.

TOM: It was great to hear him share like that.

EDDIE: He thinks he's God?

MARIE: He likes to kid around, it's a side of him people hardly ever see.

EDDIE: That was kidding?

MARIE: You didn't take him literally.

EDDIE: Of course not. Because if I did take him literally, it would be the end of our world as we know it.

MARIE: Oh, he's not vengeful.

EDDIE: Stop talking like that.

MARIE: It was a joke, Eddie. I don't believe you.

EDDIE: Can I point out that if one of the group believes he is the actual deity, it goes against the whole spirit of team-based management?

MARIE: He doesn't believe he's God. Do I have to say this? He's a very religious person. I think he feels that he talks with God, that's all.

EDDIE: Oh. Okay. Now I'm relieved. Stock tips from on high. Does this worry anybody else?

GRENDALL: Why?

EDDIE: Why? The man thinks he's God. What if people find out?

GRENDALL: What if they do?

EDDIE: Won't they question his judgment?

GRENDALL: Yes, they will. All the other venture capitalists will say, "Belmont must be crazy. Everybody knows *I'm* God, what is he thinking?"

EDDIE: You don't think this might have an impact on market confidence?

GRENDALL: It'll improve it. They love an upbeat attitude.

EDDIE: So no one sees this as a problem.

TOM: EntreBoy, where I come from this is so normal.

MARIE: Guys, go catch your planes.

GRENDALL: And guys? We never had this conversation. Bye. Bye.

(GRENDALL, EDDIE, *and* TOM *exit.*)

MARIE: O Holy Shit.

(*Lights out*)

END OF ACT ONE

ACT TWO

(BELMONT *with a microphone.* EDDIE *off to the side, waiting and watching. A large conference room.*)

BELMONT: There are things I can't say. That would be improper. The S E C would never permit it. But the Gizmo is going to change the nature, not just of human communication, but of all human contact. We will become aware of each other as never before. Time and space will be revealed as the artificial constructs they are. We will have powers such that if the ancients could see us they would hail us as gods. I know I'm going overboard. So let me just say this. I believe in this technology. I have faith in it. The people who've come with me this far, well, they've been places no one's ever been. We'll see who wants to come with me now. Now let's take a look at that demo.

(BELMONT *waves to* EDDIE *and exits. Fast forward.* GRENDALL, TOM, *and* MARIE *join* EDDIE. *The office conference room*)

EDDIE: It wasn't a road show! He was selling pieces of the true cross out there! What he's doing is insane.

GRENDALL: Literally insane? He's mentally incompetent?

TOM: He sure isn't financially incompetent, whatever he's doing, he's doing it really well.

EDDIE: He's supposed to be creating wealth. He's lying to people.

GRENDALL: Really well.

EDDIE: I stood there, I showed the technology,
he showed them this future, this—my Gizmo is not
a magic carpet, it won't get them there from here!

TOM: EntreBoy. I've never seen you lose your nerve
before.

EDDIE: Tom, it's not that—

TOM: He believes in you. That's a positive.

EDDIE: Not if he's delusional! I don't want to be
believed in by delusional people!

GRENDALL: Welcome to the New Economy.

MARIE: Eddie, are you upset because he said he's God?
Or because he says you're some kind of genius?

EDDIE: The man is entitled to his belief system, but the
S E C has rules about this stuff. Do you honestly think
we are positioned to deliver on his promises for this
product?

GRENDALL: Honestly think. Do I honestly think. You're
right. We've all been drinking a little too much of the
Kool-Aid around here—

MARIE: Eddie, he's gotten ahead of you, that's all.
He sees more potential in you than you do, even,
and that scares you, but we believe in you. Don't we.
Carbo. Don't we.

GRENDALL: If we're going to get through this, we'd
better be honest about what we are. Eddie is nothing
but—

MARIE: Now hold on—Eddie is—

GRENDALL: Eddie is what? Not an inventor—

EDDIE: So what?

GRENDALL: Not an innovator—

EDDIE: Where is this going?

GRENDALL: You are not even really a company builder—

EDDIE: That is not my job, that is your job.

GRENDALL: You are maybe an entrepreneur. Maybe. Entrepreneur wants wealth. Period. *(Beat)* Now about this God stuff. You're a regular guy, Eddie, finger on the pulse of the people. You think folks like you will be bothered by this?

EDDIE: It's not normal.

GRENDALL: Did you think he was normal? He's the fourth-richest man in America, what did you think he was?

EDDIE: Like people I know only better.

GRENDALL: And that's a common delusion where you're from?

EDDIE: Where I'm from they will think he has gone around the bend. Once they do, it's all over.

GRENDALL: Why?

EDDIE: Because he is insane, and the markets are not. I believe the markets are fundamentally rational.

GRENDALL: Then we've got nothing to talk about.

EDDIE: Why not?

GRENDALL: Because you're nuts! The market is about to value our company at upwards of thirteen billion dollars, and we still don't make anything.

EDDIE: The market is doing that on the rational assumption, based on history, that Belmont knows what he's doing.

GRENDALL: Because in the past his investments have attracted investors.

EDDIE: Because he has tricked the public into thinking his companies are viable when they aren't.

GRENDALL: Oh, for—do you really think that people are buying little bits of viable companies? They are speculating! They are buying something to turn around and sell it for a higher price to somebody else who expects to turn around and sell it for a higher price and everybody just hopes to cash out before the bubble bursts. We are not in the Gizmo-making business!

EDDIE: I know! We're in the money-making business!

GRENDALL: We are a casino! People are placing bets, and Belmont is the house! The gamblers are fading each other, and letting it ride and letting it ride, and it goes up and up until all that will be left are ever-stupider and more reckless gamblers and our stock will be held by nothing but driveling idiots, who deserve what they get, and by then we will be cashed out and gone. This market is a Ponzi scheme! A pyramid scam! Would I rather be building a real company? Yes, in the days of my youth, I had that dream. But that is not where the money is today. That is not the time we are in.

TOM: I can't hear this.

GRENDALL: Oh, now what's your problem?

TOM: I don't lie. I thought—maybe this makes me a big sucker, but—I thought I was selling something real. That's the only way I can work.

GRENDALL: Then you have a problem.

TOM: We have a problem. What if I go out there sounding different? They're going to know. 'Cause this is demoralizing.

GRENDALL: Morale is for suckers. You're not demoralized, you're disillusioned. Sooner the better.

TOM: I've been out there saying, put your money into one of the great investments of the century. The stuff sells itself. People believe me.

GRENDALL: They believe in results. We are getting results. If Belmont is a liability, we can do this without him! We can do this better without him! I set up this Potemkin company! I can run this scam!

MARIE: You're speaking mighty freely here, aren't you, Carbo?

GRENDALL: Oh, what, 'cause you're Belmont's eyes and ears and whatever other parts of him you are?

EDDIE: Watch it.

GRENDALL: Because what? She'll get me fired? Not likely. Between now and when we go public, any change in management, mission, or financial condition, and Belmont has to file a whole new prospectus and start the clock again, and that is the last thing he wants. So I will speak as freely as I like!

TOM: You're not a legend, Carbo. Come on. Belmont's a legend. It's easier for people to believe in a legend.

GRENDALL: He wasn't a legend when he started.

TOM: No, and it took him a hell of a lot of work to put a fund together, too. He was a big unknown. But the legend grew. You on the other hand are known. And that's a drawback.

GRENDALL: Being known is a drawback now?

TOM: It is when you're known for cratering your startup.

EDDIE: Haven't you heard, he didn't crater his startup.

GRENDALL: Of course I cratered my startup! And who made me crater my startup? Belmont! Who wouldn't fund me, just when I was ready to go to market?

Belmont! Who made it impossible for me to raise money anywhere, because nobody would invest in something he pulled out of? Belmont! And who got hurt? Me!

TOM: Right. He walks out of the fire and you're a crispy critter and which one would people rather invest in? You see the problem.

GRENDALL: You know what I think, I think he funded my company just to rope me into his organization! Between my underwater stock options and my non-compete agreement and my name being mud, he's got me at slave wages. I'm a slave here till we vest.

TOM: So you do see the problem.

GRENDALL: I wouldn't worry about subtle changes in your demeanor, Tom. After all, everybody you're quote selling to unquote is in Belmont's *keiretsu*. Oh. Didn't you know that?

EDDIE: Carbo. Shut up.

GRENDALL: They're buying our stuff for the same reason we give them outsourcing contracts: so the market sees us all looking busy. It's a shell game. Didn't it seem miraculously easy to close these guys? Didn't you ever wonder about that?

EDDIE: Carbo. Shut The Fuck Up.

TOM: Are you telling me they've all been sitting there, in on the joke, letting me run my mouth and thinking I'm this idiot?

GRENDALL: No, I mean they think you're in on the joke too, and you're doing the most amazing job of going through the motions.

TOM: I don't buy that. There is a belief. I see it. There is a belief.

GRENDALL: Okay.

TOM: I succeeded.

EDDIE: You did great.

TOM: That is not what he just told me. You're telling me it was all a big fake. You're saying you bought my way in. Story of my god damn life!

MARIE: Tom! Tom. Where's the list of who you've sold. Call it up.

TOM: Under the Fraud directory.

MARIE: Cut it out, Tom. Call it up. *(Pointing and clicking)* Here, I'll do it.

TOM: Damn damn damn damn damn damn...

MARIE: Tom! Listen to me. Look at the list. Most of these companies have nothing to do with us. I am sorting...chronologically...by the close dates. Tom, all the deals you've closed in the last two quarters— look at this—none of these companies is in our *keiretsu*. *(Beat)* Did I do it right? Does that look right?

TOM: No kidding?

MARIE: No kidding.

EDDIE: Way to go, man.

MARIE: Way to believe, Tom.

TOM: But what do we do now?

(Beat)

MARIE: We stay focused. Eddie. If we keep spinning, go public, get capitalized, we can put a Gizmo in every pocket. Your time will come. Tom. Keep selling that dream. We've got to keep the faith.

EDDIE: I'm trying to stay realistic.

MARIE: That may not be the most rational response to the situation.

EDDIE: You're not talking sense.

MARIE: No, I'm talking faith. Work with me, Eddie?

(Beat)

GRENDALL: We are talking about investment decisions, right? People investing money?

MARIE: Come on, Carbo. Do you really think—do you really think that all that people are investing is their money?

(Beat)

TOM: I've got a plane.

MARIE: Get on that plane, Tom.

TOM: Bye, all. *(He exits.)*

MARIE: I've got to see Himself, it's that time.

EDDIE: Marie. Good job.

*(*MARIE *exits.)*

GRENDALL: Eddie. We never had this conversation.

EDDIE: You know what? I had this conversation. This is actually happening in my life. I bet with all the conversations you've never had, you're the youngest person here. *(He exits.)*

GRENDALL: Youngest person here. I'm the youngest person here. I got my youth back! Halleluiah!

(The lights change. MARIE *joins* BELMONT.*)*

MARIE: Hey. It's that time.

(Beat)

BELMONT: My arm hurts.

MARIE: Are you all right? You want the doctor?

BELMONT: Twinge down my arm. Couple too many laps? Am I going to drop dead? I don't know. Isn't that stupid? I can predict everything but that. And if I can't predict that, if I don't know when someone will live or die, how can I do this?

MARIE: Do what?

BELMONT: This, all this.

MARIE: I don't know. But you do.

BELMONT: You know what it is? Large numbers. Large numbers. It works on a global scale. It works with populations. It doesn't work with people. Remember that.

MARIE: Okay.

BELMONT: It doesn't work with people.

(EDDIE *enters.*)

EDDIE: Mr Belmont. There you are.

BELMONT: I know.

MARIE: He may need somebody, he was—

BELMONT: I'm fine.

MARIE: You were talking about dying, if you want we could—

BELMONT: Oh, there's no way I'm going to die in the middle of a market like this. Come on. This is the most alive any of us is ever going to be. So, Fisker. Here's why I called you in.

EDDIE: You called me in? I didn't get any—

BELMONT: Of course I called you in. Why else would you be here?

EDDIE: I came to find you.

BELMONT: Of course you did. I wanted you to.

EDDIE: But—

BELMONT: Fisker, I am creating the movement of international markets, do you think I can't put it in your mind to come and see me? I don't need email, voice mail, to make my wishes known, we are pioneering a whole new level of connection here. You know that better than anyone. You're the Kid With the Gizmo! You are my prototype.

EDDIE: You wanted to see me.

BELMONT: Obviously. Here you are.

EDDIE: What about?

BELMONT: You tell me. There, you see how it works? My problem, worked out, over there, in your brain. This is the future of networking. So talk to me.

(Beat)

EDDIE: Mister Belmont, I have immense respect for you. But what I came here to say... Some of the things you've been saying about the Gizmo... They are just not true.

BELMONT: Of course they're true.

EDDIE: Sir, no—

BELMONT: Oh for Pete's sake, they're not true now. Why should I waste my time saying things that are true now? If I am going to lead, I have got to stay at least two steps ahead of the facts.

EDDIE: But, sir, if you—

BELMONT: And your job is to make what I say just as true as you possibly can. So if you dispute my claims for this product, you had better get back to work. I have faith in you. You can do it, I know you can. Can you do it, son?

(Beat)

EDDIE: Sir? Why did you pick me? Out of all the people who come to you. Why me?

BELMONT: You had that light around you. Confidence. Belief. But I've got to tell you, Fisker. You're starting to look a little dim.

EDDIE: Mister Belmont, I'm sorry, but facts are facts.

BELMONT: Oh, get out of the box!

EDDIE: I am out of the box! We are so far out of the box!

BELMONT: Do not try to make me lose faith in myself! Do you people have any idea what could happen if you make me lose faith in myself! Any idea! Everyone believes me. Everyone. Never tell me I don't know what I'm doing. Never. Is that clear?

(Beat)

MARIE: Yes. Yes.

(BELMONT exits.)

EDDIE: I feel like I've been cheating *him*. How does he do that?

MARIE: You followed me?

EDDIE: I had to see for myself.

MARIE: You should have trusted me, Eddie. You were so much happier.

EDDIE: I wish you could have...I just hope that the next time you see a guy putting his whole future into somebody's hands, if you, before the three of you get on the plane, if you could just mention to the guy if you happen to know that the somebody is a gibbering dithering cuckoo lunatic!

MARIE: That's not how he seems to me.

EDDIE: Why the hell not!

MARIE: Because I love him. To me he just is who he is. He's not like anybody else. You knew he wasn't normal.

EDDIE: I thought he was shitloads more normal than this!

MARIE: This is the only way I know him.

EDDIE: And you kept it to yourself. Or do the other guys know? Grendall? Tom? Not that he'd mind. He might not even notice.

MARIE: What was I supposed to—

EDDIE: Oh, this is so much worse than I thought! Here we all are, our little band, skipping through the Land of Oz. Yes, it's perfect, we've got one with no brain, one with no heart, one with no nerve—

MARIE: And I guess I'm Dorothy in this scenario?

EDDIE: —and there's the Wizard, with a big huge head and a big huge voice and fire spurting out all around, and lo and behold, I look behind the curtain and what do I see.

MARIE: A very sweet, ordinary man.

EDDIE: No. I see you. The great and powerful Wizard of Oz.

(Beat)

MARIE: Don't be lame.

EDDIE: Who rallies the troops? Who keeps the story straight? Is it just us Gizmo guys, or are you doing this to everybody?

MARIE: Not everybody.

EDDIE: Just the venture capital side, or the trading floor too?

MARIE: The Oompa-Loompas? No, just the venture capital.

EDDIE: So far.

MARIE: I'm just trying to help him.

EDDIE: You love him.

MARIE: I was in a bad way when he found me. Normal people, yeah, fine, you don't know. When somebody sees you at your absolute worst and says, "You look okay to me. Anybody tells you different, he's the crazy one. You're not crazy. You're great." Do you know what it means for that to be the most incredible idea you ever heard?

EDDIE: Yeah, actually.

MARIE: Oh, when did you ever need someone to say that to you?

EDDIE: Gus Belmont pretty much said that to me.

MARIE: Well then. If you owe somebody your life, what do you think that means?

(MARIE *exits, leaving* EDDIE.)

(*Lights up on* TORIA)

TORIA: While naysayers are asking how long this rocket can fly, one superstar says the sky is still the limit. I'm Toria Bruno. Join me tonight for a rare in-depth interview with the man many call the King of the Commercial Cosmos—okay, has anybody ever called him that? Right, again. This is Toria Bruno. Won't you join me tonight? Why, am I coming apart? Sorry. I'm fine. All professionals here. Toria Bruno, Toria Bruno, Toria Bruno Toria Toria Toria. Okay.

(*Lights out on* TORIA)

(TOM *enters, on the phone, holding a remote.*)

TOM: I'm sorry, I just haven't noticed any difference.

EDDIE: (*On the phone*) He's irrational, his moves are random, he has all these disproportionate reactions—

TOM: Well, hell, he's just like the stock market! No wonder he's a genius with it!

EDDIE: Oh, and you're saying this crazy market needs an analyst who's insane?

TOM: Rings true to me.

EDDIE: Oop—hang on—

TOM: Me too—

(They push phone buttons. Lights up on MARIE, *in the office, holding a remote)*

MARIE: Me. Hi. So, you watching?

EDDIE: Of course I'm watching.

TOM: Are you okay?

MARIE: Fine, I'm fine, you know how I feel about T V, that's all.

(Lights up on BELMONT *and* TORIA, *in the studio. Elsewhere,* GRENDALL, *not on the phone with anyone, is poised at his laptop.)*

TORIA: We're back. Mister Belmont—

TOM: Hey. He looks fine. Nothing to worry about.

TORIA: You are the idol of Wall Street. The Golden Bull.

MARIE: I want to kill this woman!

BELMONT: Well.

TORIA: It's true, you must know people see you as a god of this bull market. How does that feel?

MARIE: Oh no.

BELMONT: It feels...like I'd better keep working hard to justify that kind of faith.

MARIE: Good, okay...

TOM: He's doing great.

TORIA: The Dow has been down every day this week. Some analysts have started using the C-word. People are looking to you.

MARIE: Stop it, stop tempting him.

TORIA: What can you tell us? What do you see?

BELMONT: First I will tell you: do not be afraid. A new time is being created. If you see it coming toward you, the speed, the force, can be terrifying. But once you are a part of it, it all coheres.

MARIE: They're setting him up. They'll kill him.

BELMONT: I take heart from chaos theory. For all of history chaos has been seen as disorder, monstrous—but now we know, that chaos is just a more complex form of order. More beautiful, more natural. The new millennium will be the millennium of chaos. I'm glad to be a part of it.

MARIE: Can you see the Bloomberg? What are the markets doing?

TOM: Nothing yet.

TORIA: But what about the Fed raising interest rates again? Won't that have a dampening effect?

BELMONT: Why? People worry about interest rates, the price of money, the chance they can't afford the leverage they need to fund their companies. A quarter point, a half point—who cares? In the tech sector, we shrug that off. We know that Mr Greenspan and his gnomes are nothing compared to the power of the leverage we command. People, we are living Archimedes's dream. We have built platforms. We have limitless leverage. We have moved the world.

TOM: Oh my God. Look at the Nasdaq. Oh my God.

TORIA: That is...uplifting.

TOM: Literally. Look at the Dow.

TORIA: We'll be right back.

TOM: Marie, he's...I'm honored to know him.

GRENDALL: *(To nobody)* I told him that. I've been saying that forever.

MARIE: It's a feedback loop, this is bad.

TOM: What is the matter?

MARIE: It's a feedback loop, he sends signals and the market responds to them like they're facts, his positions improve, he gets more respect, they listen to him harder, he says more things, it's a feedback loop, it can't last, it'll go into spasm, this is what happens in a heart attack, the heart is a non-stop pumping and dumping machine and the rhythms of the muscles and the electrical waves from the nerves, the wires get crossed or something, it shorts out.

EDDIE: I'm not following—

MARIE: I'm sorry, I'm trying to remember stuff I got told in a hospital corridor and I didn't know I'd be tested on this material, I mean I did but I didn't think like this—

EDDIE: His heart attack. You were there, for that. I'd heard.

MARIE: And the heart bypass and all of that, listen to me. He and the markets, they are flying higher and higher and he will get prouder and prouder and the opinions will get more and more outrageous and the market swings will get bigger and bigger, and it will all melt down and fall out of the sky.

EDDIE: Like in the twenties?

MARIE: Like in the Greeks!

EDDIE: The Greek markets?

MARIE: The Greek classics, oh for the gods sakes,
why did I bother doing my homework so now nobody
knows what I'm talking about! I'm that woman.
I'm that woman, I'm the opposite of him, I'm the
one where everything I say is true and nobody listens.
Hello, Prospera Funds, this is Cassandra, how may
I direct your cries to the gods for mercy? For Zeus,
press one. For Hera, press two.

TOM: Marie, what are you on?

MARIE: What?

TOM: What pills did you take today?

MARIE: Couple kinds, I don't know, I'll be okay. Some
speed and a Quaalude, see, I'm okay, I hedged.

EDDIE: Wo.

MARIE: I'm alone and I'm scared and this phone is
giving me cancer.

TOM: Try to sleep.

(MARIE *hangs up and exits.*)

EDDIE: Marie? Marie? Tom, I gotta go.

TOM: Where you going?

EDDIE: Home.

TOM: Home? Where's that? (*He exits.*)

(*Fast forward.* MARIE *enters and sees* EDDIE.)

MARIE: You're here.

EDDIE: I got on a plane, I flew all night.

MARIE: Why?

EDDIE: You said you were scared.

MARIE: I said that? When did I say that?

EDDIE: When we were talking on the phone? When Belmont was on T V? When you were on drugs?

MARIE: Sorry sorry sorry sorry sorry.

EDDIE: What are you scared about?

MARIE: I'm fine now.

EDDIE: You are? Good. That's great. Congratulations.

MARIE: Be nice, okay?

EDDIE: Tell you what. I'll be nice and you grow the hell up. Okay? *(Beat)* I used to think my life was in the hands of a deeply disturbed old man. God, I miss those days. Then it seemed my life was being run by a not very well informed girl. I think I could have lived with that. But now I learn that the not very well informed girl is also deeply disturbed! So please! Okay?

MARIE: You want me to be less disturbed?

EDDIE: I would settle for better informed. *(Holding out a paper napkin)* Here.

MARIE: What is this?

EDDIE: Can you read my writing?

MARIE: "What if fiber network telecom enter soft computers semicon peripherals ripple construction const equip o jesus god." It's...legible.

EDDIE: There is no basis for Belmont's claims about the Gizmo. There is no basis for Belmont's claims about the tech sector. So the tech sector is insanely overvalued. The tech sector is a lot of the economy. So the whole economy is insanely overvalued. All because all of us trusted the judgment of a very few men like Mister Gus Belmont.

MARIE: Jesus.

EDDIE: Oh, those were the good old days. These days we're relying on your judgment.

MARIE: Jesus Christ!

EDDIE: Well? Aren't we?

MARIE: Oh, like I care about his fucking investors, I'm sorry, I've seen them, bunch of people thinking, "I'm not happy being rich, maybe I'll be happy if I'm filthy rich."

EDDIE: No. No no. Do you know who we were out there pitching to? Managers of pension funds. Schoolteachers, janitors, engineers. Normal people. I took a napkin, on the tray table. What if. I know how to do this. I was a junior analyst at J P Morgan. I made a living doing this.

MARIE: Eddie. Oh. You were an Oompa-Loompa.

EDDIE: I'm sorry?

MARIE: Nothing, go on.

EDDIE: *(Pointing to napkin items as he goes along)* What if something happens. What if people give up on, I don't know, fiber optics, everybody's been waiting forever for fiber optics to happen, what if they get fed up? Okay, so if fiber optics goes, then networking companies are gonna follow. So telecom takes a big hit, and that takes down enterprise software, and computers, and if computers go, there go semiconductors, peripherals, everything else, plus over here you could even expect a ripple effect through construction, construction equipment, so now it's into the old economy.... It's an avalanche. It's the Ice Age. And anything could do it. One thing goes, it could all go. It could happen any time. O Jesus God.

MARIE: Why are you telling me this?

EDDIE: An informed investor would act on this analysis. Take the right positions. Help her loved ones.

MARIE: What about the Gizmo?

EDDIE: If the Gizmo goes public before the market falls, we might have a chance. We'll lose a lot of market cap, but we just might make it. Do what you can.

(EDDIE *and* MARIE *exit in opposite directions as the lights change.* TOM *and* GRENDALL *enter, rolling luggage, on the phone.*)

GRENDALL: What's the stock doing?

TOM: I don't know.

GRENDALL: We opened and it just sat there. I couldn't watch anymore.

TOM: Maybe everybody's waiting for everybody else.

GRENDALL: This is killing me.

TOM: Why?

GRENDALL: Why? Billions are hanging in the balance!

TOM: Well, hey, in my family, whenever billions hung in the balance, we'd play the Muppet game.

GRENDALL: I'm sorry?

TOM: Always a hit at the kid's table Thanksgiving dinner, while we waited for the drugs to take hold.

GRENDALL: I am not going to play some stupid game.

TOM: It's easy, come on. Which Muppet are you?

GRENDALL: I have no idea which Muppet I am.

TOM: Eddie is Ernie. You and Eddie are completely Bert and Ernie.

GRENDALL: I want to be Oscar the Grouch.

TOM: No, trust me, he keeps singing about his rubber ducky and you wander around going *(Bert the Muppet's strangled anguished growl)* And me? I'm a cinch.

GRENDALL: You must be, who are you—

TOM: COOKIE!

GRENDALL: Of course. What about Marie?

(EDDIE enters, rolling luggage.)

EDDIE: *(On the phone)* What about Marie?

TOM: Hey, EntreBoy! Saw you on T V!

EDDIE: Any news?

GRENDALL: No news.

EDDIE: What was that about Marie?

TOM: Hey, if you show up late to the meeting, you have to catch up.

GRENDALL: Miss Piggy?

TOM: Of course not. Toria Bruno is Miss Piggy.

EDDIE: Oh, the Muppet game.

GRENDALL: Did everyone play this but me?

TOM: Were there other girl Muppets?

GRENDALL: What is Big Bird, anyway?

EDDIE: Marie is Kermit the Frog.

GRENDALL: Come on. That makes her pretty central, doesn't it?

TOM: She is our little green superego.

EDDIE: Trust me, Marie is Kermit the Frog.

GRENDALL: What about Belmont?

TOM: Well, that's obvious. Mr Belmont is the late, great Jim Hensen.

GRENDALL: He's the genius.

TOM: Yes, he is.

EDDIE: And we are fake fur and foam rubber with his hand up our ass.

GRENDALL: Well, we knew that.

TOM: Interesting news about Marie, though.

(MARIE *enters, rolling luggage.*)

MARIE: *(On the phone)* Hey.

TOM: Hey, Marie!

GRENDALL: Any news?

MARIE: No news. How can that be?

GRENDALL: Either nobody's willing to sell their shares of our stock—this would be incredibly good news—or nobody wants to buy it. That would be incredibly bad.

MARIE: Eddie? Are you here?

EDDIE: Yup. Yup yup yup.

TOM: Here. Where's here?

EDDIE: J F K.

TOM: L A X.

MARIE: Howdy neighbor, San Jose International.

ALL: Oo!

MARIE: Has everybody got the quote page loaded?

EDDIE: Yes, indeed.

GRENDALL: Lock and load.

(Beat)

MARIE: Any time now, guys.

(Beat)

EDDIE: What are you wearing?

GRENDALL: Who are you asking?

EDDIE: You, Carburetor.

GRENDALL: Nothing at all, baby.

EDDIE: Yow.

GRENDALL: That's right, naked as a jaybird at Detroit Metro Airport.

TOM: Detroit! Don't forget the Motor City!

EDDIE: What the hell are you doing in Detroit?

GRENDALL: Beats me. Layover?

EDDIE: Got to be.

MARIE: Oh my God...

ALL: What?

MARIE: CNN Airport News. Look up.

EDDIE: Oh my God.

MARIE: There's Eddie.

TOM: What are you saying, I can't—

MARIE: Read your lips!

ALL: Kid with a Gizmo!

GRENDALL: Look at the Bloomberg.

ALL: What is it, what is it?

EDDIE: Oh my—

GRENDALL: Do you see it?

TOM: I don't see it!

GRENDALL: Do you see it?

TOM: I don't see it!

ALL: Do you see it?

TOM: Sweet Baby Jesus!

GRENDALL: Yes! Fuck you all! Fuck you all! Fuck you all!

TOM: (*Cookie Monster*) Yrgrararar!

MARIE: Oh thank God. Oh thank God.

(EDDIE *quietly breaks down and sobs.*)

TOM: EntreBoy?

MARIE: Just breathe, Eddie. You can breathe now.

(*A classic '80s rock 'n' roll tune kicks in.*)

GRENDALL: Oh, my...look! Look at the screen!

TOM: What, the laptop—?

MARIE & GRENDALL: The T V, the T V!

EDDIE: It's the ad.

TOM: Oh my God, they placed the ad right after the story—

MARIE: Oh and the song!

GRENDALL: What did we have to pay to license this song?

MARIE: Worth every penny.

GRENDALL: Co-opted my youth.

TOM: Worth every goddamn cent!

EDDIE: Look at the Bloomberg!

TOM: They like us! They really like us!

EDDIE: Dance with me, Marie!

MARIE: I am, baby. Dance with me, everybody!

(*They are. The four of them, each in a different place, unknowing and unseen by each other, are moving as one.*)

TOM: People, put your hands together for Eddie and the Gizmos! Give it up, people!

EDDIE: They are giving it up! Look at it go!

MARIE: People! Spin move! On three!

TOM: What?

MARIE: One—

TOM: What are we—

MARIE: Two—

EDDIE: Spin, Tom!

MARIE: Three!

ALL: Yeah!

(The lights fade.)

*(*BELMONT *stares.* BELMONT*'s office.* MARIE *enters.)*

MARIE: It's that time.

BELMONT: Shh.

MARIE: What? *(Beat)* What?

BELMONT: Music.

MARIE: Can't hear it.

BELMONT: *(Pointing)* Look then. Up down. Slow fast.
Buy hold sell.

(Beat)

MARIE: Are you even trading anymore?

BELMONT: I don't have to change my positions.
I stand still. The world sees. It comes to me.
It's the most amazing thing.

MARIE: It's time.

BELMONT: I have to hold all this in my head.

MARIE: You have got to take the pressure down.

BELMONT: Mush pills, fog pills.

MARIE: Do you want another attack? Do you want to die? Again?

BELMONT: God. My head is killing me.

MARIE: It's killing everybody.

BELMONT: Get me something. Please.

MARIE: Here. Hold still.

(She presses his temples and either side of the nape of his neck, firmly.)

BELMONT: Not more pressure, ah—

MARIE: Hold still.

BELMONT: What are you—

MARIE: Wait. Trust me. It only works if you trust me. Now breathe. Breathe. Okay.

(She releases him. She strokes his face with her fingertips.)

BELMONT: Hm.

MARIE: How is that?

BELMONT: Better. A little better. What did you do?

MARIE: You increase the pressure from the outside until it breaks down the tensions making pressure on the inside.

BELMONT: Where did you learn that, the acupuncturist?

MARIE: The Federal Reserve.

(He chuckles.)

BELMONT: It's going to be—

MARIE: Shh.

BELMONT: This is good.

MARIE: Here.

(MARIE *holds out a pill.* BELMONT *takes it from her.*
Lights up on TORIA, *on the phone*)

TORIA: Toria Bruno for Mister Belmont.

BELMONT: I have to talk to her.

MARIE: Do you want to?

BELMONT: I have to.

MARIE: I can take it. Okay? *(On the phone)* Hi, this is
Marie, Mister Belmont didn't want you to have to leave
it on voice mail, but he'll have to call you back.

TORIA: That's nice of him.

MARIE: No problem. We're big fans of yours over here.

TORIA: Well, thanks—Marie, was it?

MARIE: That's right. What did you want from him?

TORIA: His response to Greenspan's testimony this
morning.

MARIE: Okay, I'll get back to you. *(To* BELMONT*)* See?
Nothing to it.

BELMONT: You keep saving my life, why is that?

MARIE: It's fun and educational.

(BELMONT *exits.* MARIE *dials a number.*)

MARIE: *(On the phone)* It's Marie. What'd you think of
Greenspan today?

(*Lights up on* GRENDALL, *on the phone*)

GRENDALL: Who wants to know?

MARIE: Me, I'm trying to learn.

GRENDALL: Did you see him?

MARIE: Yeah, but what do I know.

GRENDALL: Well, he was talking about the markets, saying it was getting out of hand, and I think he's being overly pessimistic like always.

MARIE: Overly pessimistic. Got it. Toria, hi, Marie from Gus Belmont.

TORIA: I'll take it. Hi, Marie, what's he say?

MARIE: Thinks Greenspan's being overly pessimistic.

TORIA: Anything I can use?

MARIE: Didn't he look like his necktie was on too tight?

TORIA: Boy, didn't he.

MARIE: Maybe he should loosen that necktie, give everybody a chance to breathe.

TORIA: Hey, that's great. Is that Belmont's line?

MARIE: Yup. Yup yup yup.

(Quick fast forward. TORIA *is in her studio.)*

TORIA: *(On the air)* Word on the Street is that Alan Greenspan's testimony today revealed an overly pessimistic stance on the markets.

*(*GRENDALL *is watching a screen.)*

GRENDALL: I said that, I've been... Huh.

TORIA: Gus Belmont of Prospera Funds, the market's reigning icon, said through a spokeswoman, "Maybe if he loosened that necktie, we'd all have a chance to breathe," clearly a reference to rumors of another Fed rate hike.

(Quick fast forward)

MARIE: *(On the phone)* Gus Belmont's office.

TORIA: *(On the phone)* Marie, Toria Bruno, what does Belmont think today's Association of Purchasing Managers' report will do to durable goods?

MARIE: Hang on. *(Speed dialing)* Hey, Carbo? What do you know about durable goods?

GRENDALL: *(On the phone)* Looks like the aerospace people are ready for liftoff.

MARIE: Toria? It's Marie.

*(*GRENDALL *points a remote.)*

TORIA: *(On the air)* Word on the Street says aerospace is cleared for a takeoff.

GRENDALL: Close enough.

*(*GRENDALL *grabs his laptop and starts typing. Quick fast forward.)*

TORIA: *(On the phone)* Marie, big ruling on biotech today, what does Belmont think of biotech?

MARIE: *(On the phone, speed dialing)* Carbo. What about biotech?

GRENDALL: *(On the phone, laptop at the ready)* Biotech is coming out of a long recuperation. *(He points the remote.)*

TORIA: *(On the air)* And this week ends a long convalescence for biotech.

GRENDALL: *(Typing giddily)* I hate when they misquote me.

(Quick fast forward)

TORIA: *(On the phone)* Marie, hi, coming out of this crazy Christmas, what does Prospera think of online retail?

MARIE: *(On the phone)* Carbo, online retail?

GRENDALL: *(On the phone and the laptop)* Love it. The dot-coms are here to stay. *(He points the remote.)*

TORIA: *(On the air)* Prospera says the dot-coms are never going away.

GRENDALL: *(Singing)* Anchors aweigh, my boys, anchors aweigh...

(Quick fast forward)

TORIA: *(On the phone)* Marie? Can you get me something on fiber optics?

(Beat)

MARIE: *(On the phone)* Carbo. Fiber optics.

GRENDALL: *(On the phone, typing feverishly)* Fiber optics, looking clear as a bell.

(Beat)

MARIE: Really?

GRENDALL: Yeah, really.

MARIE: *(On the phone)* Toria?

(Lights fade on MARIE and TORIA. EDDIE joins GRENDALL.)

EDDIE: Hey, Carbo.

GRENDALL: Hang on a sec.

EDDIE: Whatcha doing?

GRENDALL: Little day trading in fiber optics.

EDDIE: Really? How come?

GRENDALL: I just have a hunch they're in for a big gain.

(TOM enters, carrying a book.)

TOM: Hey, guys.

EDDIE: Tom? What is that?

TOM: *The Internet for Dummies.* Shut up. There's this conference? "Old Money, New Economy?"

EDDIE: That's great. You gonna learn something?

TOM: They asked me to chair it. So I thought I'd better bone up.

GRENDALL: Right, you want to get started?

TOM: Sure, where's Marie?

(MARIE *enters, quickly.*)

MARIE: Sorry sorry sorry.

(*Lights up on* TORIA, *in the studio*)

GRENDALL: Oh, here comes Toria Bruno, let's listen a sec. (*He finds the remote and points it.*)

TORIA: Startling word in the telecom sector, with the Prospera Funds predicting a weakening in fiber optics.

GRENDALL: No, no, we're not, no—

TORIA: Through a spokeswoman, Gus Belmont of Prospera Funds today called some of the major players in fiber optics, and I quote: "A bunch of lames."

(*Beat. The guys look at* MARIE.)

MARIE: It sounds so much harsher when she says it.

EDDIE: My God, look at fiber optics.

GRENDALL: (*Into his phone*) What's my position in fiber optics? Quickly! Am I long in fiber optics? Dump fiber optics now, vacate the position!

TOM: Look at that, there's gonna be blood on the floor.

EDDIE: Look at networking.

TOM: Look at telecom.

GRENDALL: Look at my portfolio! Oh my God!

EDDIE: Wo.

GRENDALL: Stop it! She didn't mean it! Stop it! (*He exits at a run.*)

(*The sound of time slowing down.* TOM *and* EDDIE *are keeping* MARIE *company. She watches the screens, very still.*)

TOM: I've been thinking.

EDDIE: Now that's funny.

TOM: Yeah. I went to Yale, you know?

EDDIE: Like I said.

TOM: Oh, stop, it's a perfectly good school.

EDDIE: Whatever you say.

TOM: Hey, I didn't want to go there. It wasn't my kind of place.

EDDIE: Where did you want to go?

TOM: Bennington, Sarah Lawrence.

EDDIE: Aren't those girl's schools?

TOM: Yeah.

EDDIE: Don't tell me you've ever had trouble getting girls.

TOM: Why? Oh, because of the money. Yeah. It all comes back to the money, huh.

EDDIE: Well, Tom, yeah it kind of does. I mean, here we all are, serving mankind and everything.

TOM: Yeah. I've been thinking about that. You guys know about my Granddad.

EDDIE: Sure.

TOM: And my folks, and the aunts and the uncles. How screwed up they all are? Pretty much spent their lives waiting for Granddad to die.

EDDIE: But you didn't do that, Tom.

TOM: And my cousins, and Carol, you know about my sister Carol and all.

EDDIE: Yeah.

TOM: How I was the one who found her body and all.

EDDIE: I didn't know that part. Jeez, Tom.

MARIE: You don't have to talk about this, Tom.

TOM: Well, so I was going to get out of there. I wasn't going to take anything from Granddad, not any of it, because, you know, I'd seen. Went to work, earned enough to pay my way to a decent school. Started sending applications. Not Yale. Hell no. Whole family had gone to Yale. Well, Granddad was furious. Mom and—no, Dad had O Ded by then—Mom was scared to death what he was going to do. But I sent off all those applications, and I waited. And every application came back.

EDDIE: You got rejections from all of them?

TOM: You don't understand. The applications came back. Some of them hadn't even been opened. Granddad got to all of them.

EDDIE: Oh my God. What happened then?

TOM: Well, then a letter of acceptance came from Yale. I hadn't even applied to Yale. It was Granddad's way of telling me.

EDDIE: So what did you do?

TOM: Went to Yale. Paid my own way, though.

EDDIE: That's a lot of money, how'd you do it?

TOM: Well, you'd never believe it, but it turns out I can sell things. I really like it, you know? Even cold calls.

EDDIE: Nobody likes cold calls. Selling to strangers.

TOM: Why? What did strangers ever do to you? It's not like they're your family or anything. Anyway, I've been thinking. I do this 'cause I like it. But you guys, you have all these goals. Wealth and stuff. And I think you guys are great, and I just want to ask: are you sure? I mean, what's your best case scenario? You make a big pile, huge pile, billions of dollars. An estate that will endure for generations. Why, though? I've got a message for you from your grandkids. Your grandkids are saying, what do you want, you really want us to turn out like Tom Xerox?

(Time resumes. GRENDALL *enters slowly.)*

TORIA: And at the closing bell, the big story is a massive correction today, six hundred and eighteen points off the Dow—

EDDIE: My God.

TORIA: The Nasdaq, which long-time traders characterized as a historic massacre—

*(*GRENDALL *pushes the remote. Lights out on* TORIA*)*

GRENDALL: *(To* MARIE, *enunciating)* Listen to me: "Fiber Optics, Looking Clear as a Bell." Is that so hard to understand? "Looking Clear as a Bell." Now: "Bunch of Lames." Hear the difference? "Bunch of Lames." "Clear as a Bell." How the hell did this happen!

MARIE: Goddamn cellular phones?

*(*GRENDALL *sobs.)*

EDDIE: Where have you been?

GRENDALL: Online, selling all the stocks I own. Owned.

EDDIE: Quick thinking.

GRENDALL: At least I got out before the bottom. Kept my losses in the six-figure level. Better than most.

EDDIE: How big were you before?

GRENDALL: The six-figure level.

BELMONT: *(Off, on the P A)* Marie. See me.

(Beat)

TOM: Anybody see a burning bush around here?

EDDIE: Marie? You want somebody to go with you?

MARIE: No. (*She does not move.*)

GRENDALL: How did you guys do?

EDDIE: I let it ride.

GRENDALL: You must have lost your shirt.

EDDIE: They'll come back up again. I'm a buy-and-hold kind of guy, really.

GRENDALL: What about you, Tom?

TOM: Oh, I don't own any stocks. It's nothing but legalized gambling, really, I don't approve of it.

GRENDALL: I can't believe you people.

BELMONT: (*Off, on the P A*) Marie. See me.

GRENDALL: You'd better go.

MARIE: No. Better if he comes to me.

TOM: Everybody got a surge protector?

EDDIE: Why?

TOM: Lightning strikes.

(BELMONT *enters.*)

BELMONT: I made you.

MARIE: Yes.

BELMONT: Dirt and sweat it took. You don't know.

MARIE: Yes.

BELMONT: You have been acting in my name.

MARIE: Yes.

BELMONT: Why did you do this? Why? Why? Everything's fallen. Every market in the world.

GRENDALL: And you fucked up my Fuck You Fund! And the Gizmo! You guys—she killed the tech sector!

The Gizmo's in the tech sector! You know what she did? She cratered our startup!

MARIE: I waited till you went public! Do you know what a risk that was? I made sure you went public first, Eddie, you said—

BELMONT: You—what?—you—

MARIE: Guys, listen—Tom, somebody—

GRENDALL: Why didn't you warn me?

MARIE: That's inside information! I'm trying to run a straight-up operation!

BELMONT: *You're* trying—

MARIE: Guys. There was nothing here. Remember? A spark of a bright idea, yes, but really, you and you and you and even you, and the amazing way you tell a good story. Isn't it something, it is the most incredible thing, how much people love a good story. They'll give anything. For a while.

BELMONT: This could have kept going forever.

MARIE: No.

BELMONT: If everyone had kept agreeing. As long as everyone agreed to keep it going, it kept going. They could have kept believing, and it would have stayed true.

MARIE: People can't do that. The same thing? People can change, they have to change. You taught me that.

BELMONT: Get out. I don't want to see you again. Get out of here.

MARIE: Gus—

BELMONT: And don't try to tell me you're sorry.

MARIE: I'm not.

BELMONT: You—I got you out of Switzerland!

MARIE: I'm trying to get you out of this!

BELMONT: Go to hell.

EDDIE: But, sir. Wait. You must have known what was going on.

BELMONT: Why the hell would I—

EDDIE: I mean, because given Who You Are... If you didn't know what was going on...Who are you?

MARIE: Eddie—

EDDIE: You must have known what Marie was doing. She didn't need to tell you. Your problem, worked out in her brain.

BELMONT: What are you, insane?

EDDIE: This was your idea. It had to be. Otherwise...

BELMONT: Why would I do that? Why? Are you all in on this?

MARIE: No, no. Just me. Plus the Oompa-Loompas.

BELMONT: The Oompa-Loompas?!?

GRENDALL: The trading floor, sir.

MARIE: I think... *(Pointing the remote)* Yes.

(Lights up on TORIA*)*

TORIA: Toria Bruno. Word on the Street is there was one big winner today: the Prospera Funds, rumored to have taken enormous short positions in all the sectors that took big hits today. Prospera predicted today's correction, and they seem to have hit the jackpot. For those of you just tuning in, this collapse began in the tech sector, with a selloff in fiber optics, followed by networking companies, which led to a meltdown in telecom, enterprise software, computers,

and semiconductors, with the beginnings of a ripple
effect through construction and construction equipment.

EDDIE: *(To* MARIE*)* I want my paper napkin back.

TORIA: This is a return to the kind of bold, visionary
move that made Gus Belmont's name.

(Beat. Everybody looks at MARIE*.)*

BELMONT: Did you know Prospera was betting that all
those sectors would fall?

MARIE: Yes.

BELMONT: Did the trading floor tell you they were
betting all those sectors would fall?

MARIE: No. I told them to. Weeks ago. They said,
"Thank God. Belmont's himself again."

TORIA: *(On the phone)* Hi, Toria Bruno for Marie?

BELMONT: "For Marie."

(Beat)

MARIE: Take it.

(Beat. BELMONT *picks up the phone.)*

BELMONT: Hey, doll.

TORIA: Mister Belmont! Wow. Congratulations.

BELMONT: Thanks.

TORIA: If the rumors are true, this is the biggest one-day
gain in Prospera Fund's history, is that true?

(Beat)

BELMONT: Really? I didn't know. We haven't finished
counting.

TORIA: You want to say anything about how you did it?

BELMONT: Well.

TORIA: Because I have to tell you, you know what a fan I am, but this, architecting this shorting strategy, oh my God, I don't know if even, well, you have read the market this well and called the shot so big.

BELMONT: Thank you.

TORIA: Any comments?

BELMONT: Absolutely. You know me.

TORIA: Can we do this on the air?

BELMONT: Hang on a moment, would you?

TORIA: Sure, I'll hold. Hook me up, we're going live!

(BELMONT *stands, head bowed.*)

MARIE: Talk to me?

BELMONT: Shh. *(Beat)* Music's stopped.

MARIE: Talk to me?

(BELMONT *raises the phone above his head, as if to smash it on the floor. Then he breathes, a long sigh. He speaks to the phone.*)

BELMONT: I'm back.

TORIA: Hey, I'll say. So—

BELMONT: Toria... The Prospera Funds are bigger than any one person by now. I've been training disciples for quite a while, and they're coming into their own. That market reading was based on my philosophy, but it was a corporate decision.

TORIA: The Gospel According to Belmont.

BELMONT: That's right. But this one was more the Acts of the Apostles. One of them is my niece, Marie. You'll be hearing more about her.

TORIA: Your niece? Marie is your niece?

GRENDALL & TOM: His niece?

EDDIE: His literal niece?

MARIE: What the hell did you think?

THE GUYS: Wo.

TORIA: You mean there's more where you came from?

BELMONT: That's right.

TORIA: One last question?

BELMONT: Shoot.

TORIA: There's been talk for a long time now, you must be aware of it, talk that you should stand for national office. Would you consider a run for the White House?

BELMONT: Well. All I'm going to say right now is... God bless America. *(He exits.)*

TORIA: Fantastic. This is Toria Bruno, saying watch what happens.

(Lights out on TORIA.*)*

TOM: Was that what happened? He was training us for this?

GRENDALL: Give him credit, he can still think on his feet when he's flat on his back.

TOM: The man was a genius.

GRENDALL: What the hell does that mean, Tom?

TOM: I don't know. Marie?

MARIE: The spirit moved him. He...occurred.

TOM: Yeah. Kind of godlike in a way. He was right about that after all, huh.

EDDIE: Not going there.

TOM: Okay, I've got a plane. By the way, do I have a job?

(Beat)

EDDIE: If you want it, you still have a job with a small, publicly held electronics company. Which is about to start building its first product. The Gizmo.

TOM: Selling something that actually exists. It's so physical.

GRENDALL: Keep the plane. I'll take the parachute. So long, all.

MARIE: Carbo. Are you sure?

TOM: Where are you going to have more fun than this?

GRENDALL: I'm thinking General Motors. Maybe the post office. *(Picking up his laptop and going)* For a minute there I almost liked you people.

EDDIE: Carbo? It's up to you, but... If you stay. Build a real company. I hear that's something people dream of doing, when they're young.

GRENDALL: This can't possibly last.

MARIE: Well, duh. As opposed to what?

TOM: Can we share a car?

GRENDALL: Probably not.

EDDIE: Come on, Carbo. What do you say?

GRENDALL: I'll call when I get there.

TOM: Good man.

MARIE: I'll miss you guys.

TOM: Miss you already.

EDDIE: What about you, Marie?

MARIE: Well. I could come with you, Eddie.

EDDIE: Me?

GRENDALL: Him?

MARIE: Yeah.

GRENDALL: Why him?

TOM: He's just a lucky guy. Come on.

(TOM *and* GRENDALL *exit.*)

EDDIE: Wo.

MARIE: Could I ask a stupid question?

EDDIE: No. I don't think you possibly could.

MARIE: I mean it. Okay: the Gizmo? What is it supposed to do?

EDDIE: Well. It's technical....

MARIE: Uh huh?

EDDIE: Basically it's what we call a platform. With a bunch of functions. To help people remember what they need to know. And let them share information. And connect people. With no wires. In real time. All in one...little place.

(*Which, by the way, is just where they are.*)

MARIE: Oh, it works. (*She kisses him.*) Come on. Keep up.

EDDIE: I'm trying, I'm trying.

MARIE: Tell me something?

EDDIE: Sure, what?

MARIE: I don't know. Make something up.

(*They exit as the lights fade.*)

END OF PLAY